AN INFOGRAPHIC HISTORY OF THE COLD WAR

ELLIOTT L. WATSON
AND
CONAL SMITH

Websites
www.versushistory.com
www.thecourseworkclub.com

Twitter:
@VersusHistory
@thelibrarian6
@prohistoricman

Instagram:
versushistory

For the Smith and Watson families, whose enduring patience allows for the creation of these kinds of things.

FOREWORD BY SAM STRICKLAND

The Cold War era is one of the most fascinating and academically inspiring periods of modern history. As a child I grew up on military bases and lived through what is termed 'the Second Cold War.' I was afforded a series of unique experiences ranging from seeing some of the latest military technology and hardware taking off from the runways of air bases, to the stark reality of being told to hide under a desk during a mock run-through of a nuclear attack. It is an era covering everything: war, power struggles, espionage, paranoia, propaganda, capitalism versus communism, brinkmanship, international flashpoints, political point-scoring and one of the most publicly declared arms races in modern human history. Quite simply it is 'liquid gold' to the historian. Yet, despite being well trodden ground, *An Infographic History of the Cold War* brings something completely unique to the field, both in its design and approach. Smith and Watson succeed in breaking down the Cold War era while retaining and respecting the historiographical complexity of this topic.

The roots of the Cold War lie deeper in the echelons of history than simply the Yalta Conference of 1945. Whilst this helped lay the foundations for a divided Europe, leading to what Churchill famously termed the Iron Curtain, the origins of this particular period of international tension are far more complex. Billy Joel's lyrics to the Cold War song, *We Didn't Start the Fire*, emphasise the unique nature of Cold War divisions by claiming these tensions are 'always burning.'

After the publication in 1867 of 'Das Kapital', by Karl Marx, intellectuals and revolutionaries began to question the integrity, relevance and virtues of an industrial-capitalist system of 'haves' and 'have nots'. The questioning of why there should be rich industrial oligarchies began to carry more weight as economies wavered and significant swathes of people suffered. William Cobbett's challenge - 'I defy you to agitate any fellow with a full stomach' - developed greater relevance in this new and industrial world. Consequently, the seeds of the Cold War were laid down in a historical divide between two ideological stances, namely communism and capitalism.

The broiling tension between communism and capitalist democracy was beautifully hidden under the banner of interwar appeasement and the subsequent fight against the Nazis. The Second World War merely served as a band-aid over the ideological cracks in the convenient wartime alliance between Mother Russia and the USA. Once the common enemy was defeated in 1945, the ideological differences between the USSR and the USA came to the fore. Stalin's disdain and mistrust of the West was magnified when the new presidential 'kid on the block', Harry Truman, assumed the chair in the White House. Truman's 'Iron Fist' approach, with the Truman Doctrine and the policy of containment, helped to shape and influence American foreign policy for most of the 20th Century.

Whilst the Cold War is often seen as a war of words, a war of propaganda, a war of personality, and a war of ideologies, there were also constant threats of imminent direct, or 'hot', fighting. Although it became apparent that a direct confrontation was not going to take place in continental Europe following the Berlin Blockade, the Cold War expanded to other theatres. Although America and the Soviet Union did not come publicly into direct conflict, there were localised proxy conflicts in Korea, Vietnam and Afghanistan. It was clear that both superpowers were keen to out-smart, out-do and out-gun the other. Arguably the closest the two opponents came to direct conflict was during the Cuban Missile Crisis. During the thirteen days of the crisis, the world held its breath as the USSR and the USA brough the planet to the brink of MAD (mutually assured destruction). The Cold War even transcended the Earth's atmosphere with a widely televised space race and a rush for the Moon.

Once Ronald Reagan became President, all bets were off. The thawing of international relations in the 1970's swiftly moved to a period of freezing once more. The Olympic Games of 1980 and 1984 were boycotted. The 'Second Cold War' gathered pace. Reagan believed, along with key White House advisors, that it was time to deliver a hammer blow to the USSR. To him, the key to winning the Cold War and defeating communism once and for all, lay in expanding America's military spending and challenging the USSR to keep pace. The financial burden of a new arms race was something the Soviet economy could not shoulder; if it tried, it would collapse. The final nail in the coffin was the SDI, or Star Wars, programme which arguably precipitated the new Soviet leader Mikhail Gorbachev's policy reforms of Glasnost and Perestroika.

The Cold War still carries much relevancy and common historical currency today. The after-effects of the collapse of the USSR and the fall of the Berlin Wall can still be seen and felt geo-politically. This is particularly visible in much of Eastern Europe, where older generations can still recall Radio Free Europe and American cinema, which has notable Cold War influences in films such as Rambo, Platoon, Predator and Aliens. Understanding this fascinating era of history is important to understanding today's world and *An Infographic History of The Cold War* will aid historians, teachers, students and general interest readers alike. This book will be a welcome addition to History Departments across the world with its use of dual coding, allowing for an engaging as well as historically academic read. It is useful for any historian of any age. Enjoy. It is a treat to behold.

Sam Strickland
Historian and Principal

PAGES OF HISTORY

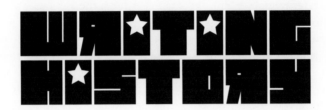

WRITING HISTORY

History is not neat. Human activity is messy; the recording of it is almost as messy. History is a woven web of infinite strands that requires the greatest of efforts not only to identify those strands but also to trace them in a manner that sensibly, honestly and truthfully shows their connections. Many students of History do not ever come close to fathoming their way through this web of human interaction; very few can say they have successfully identified the individual filaments; even fewer can claim to have understood the entire fabric. How then can we students make sense of something so seemingly inscrutable? Perhaps a complex problem requires a simple solution.

When schools and universities teach the subject of History, they tend to do so by delineation: they find ways to classify and categorise; dividing and subdividing information into consumable, understandable, 'chunks'. The learner is then more readily able to understand the history being taught. Issues of cause, consequence, and significance are often explored through such delineations precisely because they are *easier* to deliver and assimilate. It is through these selected delineations – of which there are many (time period, theme, rise/fall and so on) – that the interminably complex weave of the infinite number of contributing factors affecting how History is perceived and recorded, can be understood. Since History cannot always be measured in the same way the Natural Sciences are able to measure the physical world, perhaps the way forward is to, *at first*, simplify. Once simplified and understood, students of History can then take their understanding of a topic and build upon it – the way an intricately-designed house might be constructed upon the most rudimentary of foundations. Our second book in the *Infographic* series was written to accomplish this very end.

Every other page of *An Infographic History of the Cold War* contains a free-to-download high-quality infographic that distils some of the details of key issues within the history of this period. Each infographic is accompanied on the opposite page by an overview of the issue being dealt with, a sophisticated (but brief) explanation as to its significance, an example of historiography which has been selected for its thought-provoking and enlightening nature, as well as some suggestions for further exploration of the topic.

The timeline infographic which starts opposite (and can be downloaded using the QR Code/URL on this page) is an example of how a significant stretch of complex history can be 'delineated'. Although we do our best, history is complex and does not always adhere neatly to chapters in a book. Consequently, there will always be a little 'untidiness' in the chapter divisions we establish within the following pages. We ask your understanding if you encounter any of this 'untidiness'.

We hope our second in the *Infographic* series helps make sense of the Cold War in some way.

A big thank you to Sam Strickland for writing the foreword to this book, and to Kate Jones for being a constant source of support.

Elliott & Conal

bit.ly/3Ioo45t

PART 1

Cold War Timeline
1943-1991

Nov/Dec 1943	February 1945	July 1945	July 1945	1945

Tehran Conference

Yalta Conference

Germany: Zones of Occupation

Potsdam Conference

Soviet Takeover of Eastern Europe Begins

www.versushistory.com @versushistory

PART 2

Cold War Timeline
1943-1991

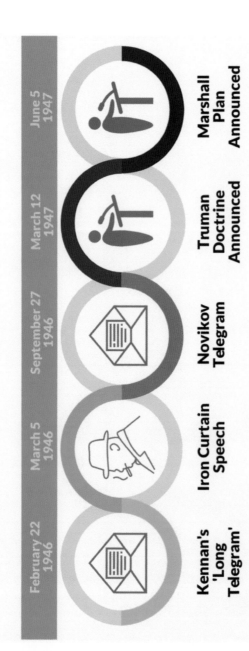

February 22 1946 — Kennan's 'Long Telegram'

March 5 1946 — Iron Curtain Speech

September 27 1946 — Novikov Telegram

March 12 1947 — Truman Doctrine Announced

June 5 1947 — Marshall Plan Announced

www.versushistory.com   @versushistory

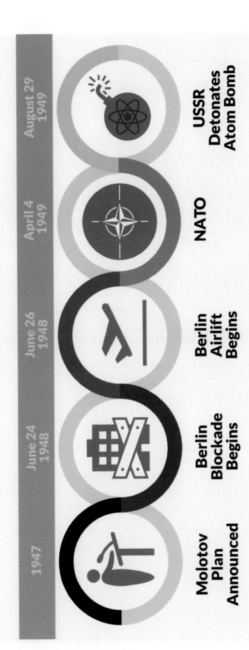

PART 3

Cold War Timeline
1943-1991

1947	June 24 1948	June 26 1948	April 4 1949	August 29 1949
Molotov Plan Announced	Berlin Blockade Begins	Berlin Airlift Begins	NATO	USSR Detonates Atom Bomb

www.versushistory.com   @versushistory

PART 4

Cold War Timeline
1943-1991

October 1 1949	June 25 1950	July 27 1953	May 14 1955	Oct/Nov 1956
China Becomes Communist	North Korea Invades South Korea	Armistice Signed	Warsaw Pact Created	Hungarian Uprising

www.versushistory.com   @versushistory

PART 5

Cold War Timeline
1943-1991

1959	May 1 1960	April 1961	June 4 1961	October 1961

Cuban Revolution

U2 Shot Down

Bay of Pigs

Vienna Summit

US Troops Arrive in Vietnam

www.versushistory.com @versushistory

PART 6

Cold War Timeline
1943-1991

| October 22 1962 | June 26 1963 | August 20 1968 | July 20 1969 | September 28 1970 |

Cuban Missile Crisis Begins

JFK Visits West Berlin

Warsaw Pact Invades Czechoslovakia

Man Lands on the Moon

Gamal Abdel Nassar of Egypt Dies

www.versushistory.com @versushistory

PART 7

Cold War Timeline
1943-1991

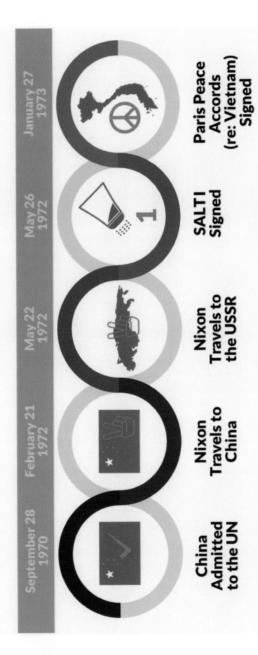

September 28 1970	February 21 1972	May 22 1972	May 26 1972	January 27 1973
China Admitted to the UN	Nixon Travels to China	Nixon Travels to the USSR	SALT I Signed	Paris Peace Accords (re: Vietnam) Signed

www.versushistory.com   @versushistory

PART 8

Cold War Timeline
1943-1991

September 12 1974	April 30 1975	July 1975	August 1 1975	December 25 1979
Haile Selassie of Ethiopia Removed by Soviet-Backed Coup	North Vietnam seizes Saigon	Apollo-Soyuz Mission	Helsinki Accords	The USSR Invades Afghanistan

www.versushistory.com   @versushistory

PART 9

Cold War Timeline
1943-1991

August 31 1980	January 20 1981	September 1 1983	March 11 1985	1987

Solidarity is Formed in Poland

Ronald Reagan Becomes President

USSR Shoots Down South Korean Airliner

Gorbachev Becomes General Secretary of the Communist Party

Gorbachev Announces 'New Thinking'

www.versushistory.com @versushistory

PART 10

Cold War Timeline
1943-1991

February 8 1988	October 23 1989	November 9 1989	December 2 1989	December 26 1991

Gorbachev Withdraws Troops from Afghanistan

Hungary Announces Democracy

East Germany Opens Border to West Germany

The USSR and USA Announce End of Cold War

The USSR Ceases to Exist

www.versushistory.com   @versushistory

ORIGINS OF THE COLD WAR 1943-49

THE POLAR FREEZE

OVERVIEW

Although the *term* 'cold war' predates what we have come to know as *the* Cold War, it is worth noting some of its origins. Mentioned by George Orwell in his essay *You and the Atomic Bomb,* as well as in a piece he wrote in *The Observer* newspaper, the term was a general one that postulated a permanent state of 'cold war' between countries living under the constant threat of nuclear warfare. American Bernard Baruch was the first to use the term in direct relation to the post-war world which saw the USSR and the USA in ideological and geopolitical confrontation, in a 1946 speech written by journalist Herbert Swope. The term became more popularly known when, tracing its origin to a French term of the 1930's – *la guerre froide* – Walter Lippman discussed the contemporary polarised global world, in his 1947 book *The Cold War.* This Cold War lasted until the collapse of the USSR and its control of Eastern Europe after 1989.

SIGNIFICANCE

The impact of the Cold War cannot satisfactorily be explained in a one paragraph analysis. Consequently, the reader is asked to indulge the broad strokes with which some of the following portrait is painted. It is no exaggeration to suggest that during 1947-1989 there was very little in the way of international relations that was not shaped, in one way or another, by the Cold War context. In a post 1949 world, in which the ever-present spectre of nuclear war haunted the human race, victory had to be measured by different metrics: proxy wars that ruined countries were veils behind which superpower rivalries played out; new forms of 'imperialism' divided the world between the USSR and the US; espionage fuelled paranoia but also technological development; trillions, was spent on militarisation. When it was all over, the 'order' created by the polarisation of the world collapsed and had to be remade in a new form – the effects of which are still being felt today.

HISTORIOGRAPHY

"As the Cold War continued, it became a struggle not just between two political and military powers but between two ways of life… Even the quality of American and Soviet kitchens and what that represented could be part of the debate."

Walter Lippmann
The Cold War: A Study in US Foreign Policy

WHERE TO FIND OUT MORE

In Confidence: Moscow's Ambassador to Six Cold War Presidents
Anatoly Dobrynin

Red Hangover: Legacies of Twentieth-Century
Kristen Ghodsee

bit.ly/3gw8xqr

WHAT WAS THE COLD WAR?

@versushistory

www.versushistory.com

The Cold War was an ideological conflict between the USA and the Soviet Union from 1945-1991, in which each country threatened to go to war, but never 'officially' fired a single shot directly at one another

Cold War Deaths

c.11 million

No. of people who died during Cold War conflicts. This number is conservative

Détente

French word meaning 'a relaxation of tension'. In the context of the Cold War it refers to times when the USSR and the USA became less hostile to one another -
when the Cold War 'thawed', e.g. the Apollo-Soyuz space mission

Length of the 'Iron Curtain'

6,779 km

Flashpoints:
times when the Cold War threatened to 'heat up' into an actual war between the US & the USSR

Proxy Wars:
conflicts that were 'sponsored' by the USSR & the USA. Because of M.A.D., wars such as that in Korea became the battlegrounds of the superpowers

God

The US added the phrase, '...under God' to the Pledge of Allegiance, in part so that Americans could stand in religious opposition to the atheism of communism

Militarisation of the World

When 12 western countries created the military alliance NATO in 1949, the USSR responded by creating the Warsaw Pact in1955. As a result, much of the world became part of the military strategies of the USA & the Soviet Union

Nuclear Weapons

125,000
No. of warheads built since 1945

97%
Built by the USA & Russia

64,500
Peak no. of warheads in existence at one time (1986)

2105
Total no. of detonations by the US and Russia, since 1945

#VersusHistory

HOW AMERICA GOT HER GROOVE BACK

OVERVIEW

Although the US was one of the Allied forces during World War Two, there had not been – other than the Japanese attack at Pearl Harbor – fighting on American soil. The American government had been reluctant to enter the war, militarily speaking, until it was given little option by the Japanese attack. Consequently, when the US entered the war, she had enjoyed the better part of two years during which time her undamaged agricultural and industrial infrastructure supplied the massive war-demands of other countries. There is little controversy to be found in the assertion that access to opening war markets dragged the US out of the Great Depression and helped ultimately remould her as the wealthiest country in the world. Wealthy enough to provide loans to other, less fortunate countries. More than this, once she became an active participant in the war, the desire for victory drove American technological innovation in both its military and industrial sectors, developing new methods of production and battle that would reshape the post-war world. In short, the US became the wealthiest and most powerful country the world had ever seen.

SIGNIFICANCE

Much of the world owed a financial debt – in one form or another – to the United States. The settling of those debts by countries also ravaged by war could be completed in a number of ways: repayment in monies; repayment in resources; repayment in 'favours'; repayment in loyalty. All of these transactions gave America an influence around the world – now a Cold War world – it had never wielded previously. Military bases were placed around the world by 'invitation' of the host countries, markets opened to American goods, and political leaderships sympathetic to American global leadership were established and supported. On top of all of this, the US had the atomic bomb. America emerged from World War Two independently wealthy (half of the world's GDP resided within her borders) and militarily untouchable. Its power and influence were unrivalled.

HISTORIOGRAPHY

"The US was by far the world's strongest nation... hesitant to assume a commanding... position. It took years to accept the need to garrison GIs in Europe and Asia... and to build an intelligence capability that offered more than amateurish adventuring."

Dr. Derek Leebaert
The Emergence of the United States as a Superpower after World War II

WHERE TO FIND OUT MORE

The Wages of Destruction
Adam Tooze

From Colony to Superpower: U.S. Foreign Relations since 1776
Professor George C. Herring

bit.ly/2DAA77y

The World's First Superpower: America Emerges from World War Two

GNP

Gross National Product (a measure of all goods and servies produced in the US) rose from $200 Billion in 1940 to $300 Billion in 1950

War-stimulated industries

Industries that were driven by war continued to expand after the war. From television to aviation, industries boomed

Global military presence

Once the war was over, America retained military bases in many parts of the world, e.g. Japan. This created a global security network never seen before

The Atom Bomb

The Manhattan Project developed the atom bomb, thus creating the world's first nuclear power. America became the most powerful country in the world

#VersusHistory

www.versushistory.com
@versushistory

War Deaths
300,000

America 'only' suffered this many deaths during the war - the lowest of any of the major belligerents

The GI Bill
1944

The federal government provided money for returning soldiers to use for their future

Destruction
1939-45

Other than at Pearl Harbor, there had been no fighting on American soil. This meant that the US did not suffer the same levels of infrastructural destruction as other countries

Employment
Public to private

Unemployment dropped to almost zero during the war as the gov't spent huge sums on war production. When the war ended, industries swiftly changed to private production. This kept unemployment at bay: 3.9% in 1947

CAUSING PROBLEMS

OVERVIEW

When discussing the causes of the Cold War, there appears to be a vast number from which to choose: there are long-term causes such as the rise of Bolshevism in Russia at the beginning of the twentieth century or the provision of 'anti-Red' US aid during the post-revolution Civil War; there are short term causes such as the replacement of FDR with Truman in 1945; there are causes somewhere in between. Fear not, what makes History a wonderful subject to study is its very multicausality. Read on.

SIGNIFICANCE

The rationale behind the actions of any state in their foreign policy is best understood from, as Yong-Soo Eun discussed (see below), a multicausal and multimethodological perspective. The complexities of motivation, need, and strategy, coupled with the resources that a country has available to deliver on them, result in an interpretation of international relations that must seek out a web of causes. Since the Cold War affected every state in the world in one way or another, it therefore involved an almost unfathomable number of motivations, needs, and strategies. Whilst this makes the Cold War – and what brought it into being – one of the most interesting periods of recent history, it also makes it one of the most complex. In a certain sense, any study of *why* the Cold War came into being is a thankless task, as there are just so many fully justifiable causes and reasons. However, the most important thing to learn about the Cold War – indeed any event in history – is to be mindful that, while one cause may be more influential than another, they are all – to one degree or another – linked.

HISTORIOGRAPHY

"The facts… are like fish swimming about in a vast and sometimes inaccessible ocean; and what the historian catches will depend, partly on chance, but mainly on what part of the ocean he chooses to fish in and what tackle he chooses to use – these two factors being, of course, determined by the kind of fish he wants to catch. By and large, the historian will get the kind of facts he wants. History means interpretation."

E.H. Carr
What is History?

WHERE TO FIND OUT MORE

Why *and* How Should we go for a Multicausal Analysis in the Study of Foreign Policy
Yong-Soo Eun

The Causal Web
Elliott L. Watson (bit.ly/3a89GlD)

bit.ly/2ETqMIA

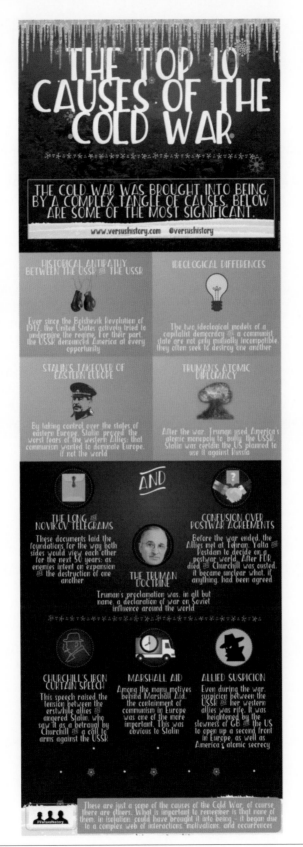

AGREEING TO DISAGREE

OVERVIEW

Once the US entered World War Two, coordination between the Allied powers became a key strategy consideration. To this end, a stream of meetings was held around the globe in the years 1943-45 in locations as varied as Casablanca, Bretton Woods in New Hampshire, and Tehran. Initial meetings focussed on the conduct of the war itself, and particularly the opening of a 'second front' against Germany, but later meetings sought to establish agreements about the shape of the post-war world, including the establishment of the United Nations.

SIGNIFICANCE

It was the later conferences, particularly that at the Crimean resort town of Yalta in February 1945, which highlighted the pressure points that would shape tension and conflict throughout the Cold War. That Europe was seen as a chessboard to be competed over for influence, was indicated by the 'percentages deal' struck by Stalin and Churchill. The Soviet desire for security and reparations, which would characterise policy towards Eastern Europe and Germany, was present in Soviet territorial demands over Poland and the Far East, while the announcement by Truman of America's atom bomb foreshadowed the arms race. How these areas of tension were to develop was far from clear in 1945, yet for historians the story of so many Cold War crises begins with the decisions taken by the 'big three' at these conferences.

HISTORIOGRAPHY

"Within a few short years at the end of the (Yalta) conference, the high hopes of its authors were dashed, their decisions condemned by friend and foe alike…Feelings of disappointment and regret dominated on both sides of the Cold War divide. Yalta became a symbol of lost opportunity, however differently perceived."

S. M. Plokhy
Yalta: The Price of Peace

WHERE TO FIND OUT MORE

Eight Days at Yalta: How Churchill, Roosevelt and Stalin Shaped the Post-War World
Diana Preston

The Allies: Roosevelt, Churchill, Stalin and the Unlikely Alliance That Won World War II
Winston Groom

bit.ly/2PEykAV

THE 'BIG 3' CONFERENCES

After the war, I want...

USSR GB USA

TEHRAN, 1943

CONTEXT
1) US and the UK had still not opened a 'second front'
2) Churchill despised the Bolsheviks
3) Katyn massacre of Polish men by the USSR discovered
4) FDR unwell

YALTA, 1945

CONTEXT
1) US and UK had opened a 'second front' in 1944
2) 17 million Russians dead fighting the Nazis
3) Allied victory imminent
4) FDR detriorating rapidly

POTSDAM, 1945

CONTEXT
1) The US had 'secretly' created an atom bomb
2) The Red Army occupied countries in the east
3) Attlee replaced Churchill
4) Truman replaced FDR

AGREEMENTS

* GB and USA agree to open a 'second front'

* USSR agrees to assist in the fight against Japan after Germany defeat

* UN should be set up after the war

* Countries of Eastern Europe should have representative governments

* Germany and Berlin to be split into 4 occupation zones

* USSR will receive part of Eastern Poland

* Germany was to be demilitarised and must pay reparations

* Poland received large parts of east Germany and began expelling Germans

* 'Potsdam Declaration' threatened Japan and called for immediate surrender

DISAGREEMENTS

TEHRAN

Churchill wanted to attack the Axis powers through the Baltic states. Stalin rejected this outright because it would threaten the secuirty of the USSR.

YALTA

Stalin refused to recognise the demands of the Polish government in exile - the London Poles. Stalin was determined to decide the fate of Poland.

POTSDAM

Now that Germany had surrendered, Stalin had begun occupying Eastern Europe, and Truman refused to share atomic secrets, the 'Big Three' disagreed on practically every issue.

www.versushistory.com @versushistory

SPACE INVADERS

OVERVIEW

As Stalin's Red Army pushed the forces of fascism westwards back across Europe from whence they had originally come, they themselves remained in those liberated countries as occupiers. Slice by slice of 'salami', Stalin's takeover of each country followed a similar pattern: these 'liberated' countries were quickly implanted with communist governments controlled by the Kremlin. From Czechoslovakia to Poland, Hungary to Bulgaria, the countries of Eastern Europe bore witness to a brutish control of their own militaries, press, police forces, and radio and television stations, by a Soviet Union intent on creating within their sphere of influence a 'buffer zone' against potential attack from the west. As far as possible, the occupied states would follow the centralised political and economic model of the Soviet Union, excepting that these states existed primarily for the sustenance of the 'mother country': the USSR.

SIGNIFICANCE

Ironically, since it was Churchill who decried that the Soviet takeover of Eastern Europe had drawn an 'iron curtain' across Europe, he was partially responsible for the metallic drapery. At the 1945 Anglo-Soviet summit in Moscow, Churchill introduced what became known informally as the 'percentages agreement'. Scrawled on a piece of paper, this secret agreement between Stalin and Churchill helped decide what the spheres of influence of their respective countries would be once the war was over. Much of Eastern Europe was ceded to Stalin, while much of southern Europe and the Mediterranean went to Britain. Nevertheless, coupled with Allied intervention in Western Europe, the takeover of Eastern Europe by the Soviet Union helped create two gigantic geo-political monoliths that faced off against one another for the duration of the Cold War.

HISTORIOGRAPHY

"In the eyes of the Russians, the numerous foreign invasions which their country has been forced to meet provide adequate justification for a policy of active intervention in Eastern Europe."

C.E. Black
Soviet Policy in Eastern Europe

WHERE TO FIND OUT MORE

Iron Curtain: The Crushing of Eastern Europe
Anne Applebaum

Stalin and the Cold War in Europe
Gerhard Wettig

bit.ly/3flwDNo

SLICING SALAMI: How Stalin took control of Eastern Europe

www.versushistory.com @versushistory

WHAT?

Salami tactics is a term first used in the 1940's to describe how the Communist Party in Hungary had taken control over the country's non-communist parties by "cutting them off like slices of salami"

Stalin utilised 'salami tactics' when taking control of the countries of Eastern Europe. He divided and conquered different political elements within each country so that, by the time it became clear what his overall plan was, it was too late – there was virtually no group left to oppose him

SLICE 1   LEAVE THE RED ARMY BEHIND

Stalin's Red Army had pushed the Nazis back through the countries of Eastern Europe. After 'liberating' these countries from Nazi control, Stalin ensured that he left his Red Army behind

Stalin believed that he had the right to control any territory held by his Red Army. Thus, the military occupation of the countries of Eastern Europe had already begun before the Nazis had even surrendered

SLICE 2   SET UP COALITION GOVERNMENTS

Stalin supported the communist parties within the countries of Eastern Europe. He then encouraged them to become part of coalition governments, alongside other parties

Once in government, the communists would begin eroding the influence of the other parties and start passing legislation in their own interest

SLICE 3   ARREST OPPOSITION

Once these Soviet-supported communist parties gained sufficient power in government, they began to order the arrest of any and all opposition leaders

In this way, each government became a communist government without political opposition. In effect, each country in Eastern Europe became a one-party communist state

SLICE 4   TAKE OVER THE KEY MECHANISMS OF CONTROL

The communist governments would then take control over those elements within a country that can be used to control the people:

The press, the media, energy industries, trade unions, transportation networks and so on

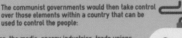

N.B.

It is important to remember that, in addition to these tactics – which were vital to the establishment of Stalin's control in the countries of Eastern Europe – there were many people who welcomed communism and Soviet influence

SLICE 5   HOLD RIGGED ELECTIONS

When the Soviet-backed communist parties were established in government, they would hold elections in order to gain the appearance of legitimacy

These elections were always rigged in favour of the communist parties already in government. Unsurprisingly, they would always win these elections with landslide victories

THE DON OF DRAPERS

OVERVIEW

Within 6 months of Japan's defeat in the Pacific, the nascent Cold War received an injection of tension when Winston Churchill delivered his, now famous, speech decrying how an "… iron curtain has descended across the continent". After leading Great Britain to victory over the forces of fascism in Europe, Winston Churchill was unceremoniously dumped out of office when his Conservative Party lost in a landslide general election to the Labour Party. Out of office, Churchill was in high demand on the 'speaking circuit'. And so it was that an invitation to speak at Westminster College in Fulton, Missouri the following year was extended. During his speech – given on 5th March – Churchill claimed that the USSR had created a permanent division of Europe, with communism in the East and the democracies in the West. Churchill, ever the orator, named this division an 'iron curtain'.

SIGNIFICANCE

There are few speeches in modern history that can claim to have been so revealing of a particular era, as well as so instrumental in bringing that era into existence. Churchill's 'Iron Curtain' speech is one of those few. While those two words – 'iron curtain' – are what posterity has chosen to record in the popular imagination, it was the rest of the speech that was simultaneously revealing of, and impactful on, the early Cold War. With Truman in attendance, Churchill looked to push for a closer relationship between the US and Britain in the face of, what he saw as, an inevitable new global polarisation of power. To Churchill, Hitler and Nazi Germany had merely been replaced by Stalin and Soviet expansion. He warned that any appeasement by the "English-speaking world", such as that which had given way to Nazism before the war, would lead to similar conflict. The speech left the required impression on the political leadership of the US, but it also put the final nail in the coffin of the Grand Alliance. For his part, Stalin called the speech "imperialist racism" and "war mongering", convincing him that the West was now a unified threat to the USSR.

HISTORIOGRAPHY

(Churchill was) "*more able to promote the desired change in American foreign policy, or perhaps better to say, to legitimize the change already in process, than any other human*".

Henry B. Ryan
A New Look at Churchill's Iron Curtain' Speech

WHERE TO FIND OUT MORE

Our Supreme Task: How Winston Churchill's Iron Curtain Speech Defined the Cold War
Philip White

The 'Sinews of Peace' speech
HD Video of the Speech: bit.ly/2UMux7S

bit.ly/30GeQIS

CHURCHILL'S IRON CURTAIN SPEECH

On March 5th 1946, former Prime Minister, Winston Churchill delivered his famous 'Iron Curtain' speech to those gathered at Westminster College in Fulton, Missouri. Despite the address actually being entitled the 'Sinews of Peace', it has become more famously known for his statement that Europe had been divided from Stettin in the north to Trieste in the south, by an 'Iron Curtain', behind which the Soviet Union controlled the ancient capitals of Eastern Europe.

1 STETTIN: POLAND

- Churchill described the 'Iron Curtain' as beginning in the city of Stettin, which is in Poland.

2 TRIESTE: ITALY

- According to Churchill, the 'Iron Curtain' stretched, unbroken, south across the continent as far as Trieste in north east Italy.

3 BERLIN: GERMANY

- Although the 'Iron Curtain' split Germany into two parts – east and west – it did the same to her capital: Berlin.

- Berlin found itself deep in the heart of Soviet-controlled East Germany, but divided between the western Allies and the USSR.

- Thus Berlin found itself at the frontline of the Cold War; it was the closest contact point between communism and capitalist-democracy.

4 STALIN'S RESPONSE

- Stalin was furious at Churchill, calling him a firebrand and comparing him to Hitler.

- Stalin claimed Churchill was intent on waging war on non English-speaking peoples.

- Stalin countered Churchill's assertions by claiming his actions in Eastern Europe were defensive and friendly in nature.

www.versushistory.com
@versushistory

COMMUNICATING CONFLICT

OVERVIEW

The Cold War evolved out of a complex form of dualism that saw both the US and USSR act and counteract one another in line with their opposing global ambitions. These ambitions were shaped by, among other things, their ideological and strategic motivations, their specific understanding of history, the actions of individual people, as well as accident and misunderstanding. It is therefore fitting, given the dualism that propelled the Cold War, that two of the most significant generators of US and Soviet Cold War policy were 'reflections' of one another. Almost as soon as the Cold War ended, both the USSR and the USA sought to interpret and evaluate one another's foreign policies. George Kennan, the US Ambassador in Moscow, delivered his interpretation of the USSR's in 1946, and Nikolai Novikov, Kennan's opposite number in Washington, issued his later that year. The format for both of these assessments was the email of the day: telegrams. Each sent telegrams to their respective governments for policy consideration.

SIGNIFICANCE

The significance of these two telegrams to the evolution of the Cold War cannot be overstated. In many respects, these two missives provided 'interpretations of the enemy' that remained largely intact for the entirety of the Cold War. Both saw one another's state as inherently expansionist and looking to destroy, existentially, the way of life of the other. Consequently, almost every policy pursued thereafter – from containment to the Vietnam War, from the Warsaw Pact to the invasion of Afghanistan – existed in the long shadows cast by these two profoundly formative analyses. Perhaps the greatest controversy surrounding the 'Long' and the 'Novikov' telegrams is how accurate an interpretation they provided of their opponent and their global ambitions. As ahistorical as it might be, just imagine how much of the Cold War might have been determined by two faulty interpretations?

HISTORIOGRAPHY

"Both the Kennan and Novikov documents are highly significant for what they reveal about the foreign policies of the United States and the Soviet Union and about how each of these countries perceived the other at the onset of the Cold War."

Viktor L. Mal'kov
Diplomatic History

WHERE TO FIND OUT MORE

Realities of American Foreign Policy
George F. Kennan

Who started the Cold War?
Versus History Podcast

bit.ly/3ka8jaZ

COLD WAR COMMUNICATIONS

'LONG' TELEGRAM FAQ NOVIKOV TELEGRAM

WHO?

GEORGE KENNAN	NIKOLAI NOVIKOV
The American Charge d'Affaires in Moscow. Career diplomat. Helped establish the first US embassy in the USSR.	Soviet Ambassador to Washington. Career academic and Russian diplomat.

WHAT?

8,000 WORDS	THE SOVIET RESPONSE
A 'long' telegram sent by Kennan from the US Embassy in Moscow to the Department of State in Washington D.C.	Much like Kennan's telegram, this was a personal interpretation for his superiors, but of US foreign policy after World War Two.

WHEN?

FEBRUARY 22, 1946	SEPTEMBER 27, 1946
Received at precisely 3:52pm by the US Department of State.	It was only declassified and released in 1990 under the Glasnost period of openness.

WHY?

AN URGENT WARNING	AN URGENT WARNING
"Wherever...efforts will be made to advance official limits of Soviet power." "...communism is like a malignant parasite which feeds only on diseased tissue."	"The foreign policy of the United States is conducted now in a situation that differs greatly from the one that existed in the prewar period.."

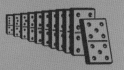

SIGNIFICANCE?

RESISTANCE	RESISTANCE
It helped establish a US foreign policy determined to resist, with force if necessary, any attempt at Soviet expansion. It underpinned the US Cold War policy of containment.	Like the 'Long Telegram', Novikov's view of the new postwar world saw the need for immediate action against the encroachment of a perceived enemy.

WWW.VERSUSHISTORY.COM @VERSUSHISTORY

'TRU' FRIENDSHIP

OVERVIEW

On March 12, 1947 President Truman gave a speech to the US Congress in which he delivered the consequential lines, "…it must be the policy of the United States to support free peoples who are resisting attempted subjugation by armed minorities or by outside pressures". World War Two had ended two years previously so Truman was not speaking about the forces of fascism; he was implicitly referencing communism as the 'subjugating' force. The war had weakened many countries of Europe, some of which had come under threat from communist insurgencies looking to gain power. Two of these were Greece and Turkey. When the British, who had been supporting their governments with financial aid, could no longer afford to do so, the Americans stepped in. The principle upon which the Truman Doctrine was founded was Dean Acheson's 'domino theory', whereby if one state should fall to communism then its neighbours would also likely fall. The US government worried that, if Greece and Turkey 'fell', then communism would likely spread to Iran and beyond. The solution to containing the spread was enunciated in the Truman Doctrine.

SIGNIFICANCE

Though he never mentioned the USSR explicitly, and only once referred to 'Communists', Truman's 'doctrine' was clearly directed at the Soviet Union; it was as much a threat to the Kremlin as it was a promise to help those being 'subjugated'. As a result, the Truman Doctrine was perhaps the first overtly confrontational declaration made by one superpower to the other in the Cold War. In a sense, the Truman Doctrine was both a cause and consequence of the Cold War: it helped drive confrontation with the Soviet Union but it was also a reflection of the ideological geopolitics already being played out in Europe. Coupled with the Marshall Plan, the Truman Doctrine introduced the policy of containment and helped draw Cold War battle lines; it shaped the nature of the nascent conflict and, predictably, led the USSR to respond in kind.

HISTORIOGRAPHY

"Did the United States correctly read Soviet intentions, exaggerate the threat, or pursue its own political and economic hegemony?"

Dennis Merrill
The Truman Doctrine: Containing Communism and Modernity

WHERE TO FIND OUT MORE

The First Cold Warrior: Harry Truman… and the Remaking of Liberal Internationalism
Elizabeth Edwards Spalding

Was the Truman Doctrine a Real Turning Point?
John Lewis Gaddis

bit.ly/3i2mhK2

Containing the spread of communism

THE TRUMAN
DOCTRINE

"I believe that it must be the policy of the United States to support free peoples who are resisting attempted subjugation by armed minorities or by outside pressures. I believe that we must assist free peoples to work out their own destinies in their own way."

President Truman

WHY

introduce the Truman Doctrine?

The 'Long Telegram'	Stalin's Takeover of Eastern Europe	Communist Threats in Greece & Turkey
George Kennan's 'Long Telegram' convinced the US State Department that Soviet communism was intent on global domination	By doing this, Stalin seemed to 'prove' the fears of America to be correct - that Soviet communism wanted world domination	Greece and Turkey were on the 'frontline' of communist insurgency. If these countries 'fell' then the rest of Europe would follow

This was the foundation of the policy of containment

When Stalin claimed 'defence', the West saw 'offence'

The domino theory emerged

US policy would interpret any Soviet action as aggressive

...countries 'fell' to Stalin. The TD stated no more would be 'lost'

Falling 'dominoes' would threaten the Middle East

Western Europe HAD to be strengthened

Marshall Aid was the solution to stop the 'spread': $13 billion

$513 million given to Greece & Turkey

What were the

CONSEQUENCES?

Marshall Aid to Europe

Communism remained where it already existed

Cold War tension rose

Containment became a global Cold War policy

The USSR felt threatened

The USSR created their own versions of the Marshall Plan & Truman Doctrine

It destroyed the wartime alliance between the US & the USSR

www.versushistory.com   @versushistory

#VersusHistory

FINANCIAL PLANNING

OVERVIEW

Also known as the European Recovery Program, the Marshall Plan was the practical arm of the Truman Doctrine. Whereas Truman's proclamation asserted the broad aims of the US containment policy, Marshall Aid helped deliver on them. Named after the man who devised it, Secretary of State George C. Marshall, the Plan aimed to help rebuild countries of Europe that had been devastated by the war. The aid and technical assistance that was delivered was not given out of simple American benevolence; there was a complex mix of motives at play. A reconstructed Europe would open markets for American goods and any country accepting US aid would also have to accept certain stipulations, like ensuring democratic elections or allowing an American military base on their soil. Prosperous countries allied to the US would be less likely to turn to communism. In short, the Marshall Plan became the vanguard of the early containment policy, as $17 billion was transferred over the duration of the Plan's lifetime (1948- 1952) to countries of Europe that then formed a 'buffer' against the spread of communism.

SIGNIFICANCE

In addition to being perhaps the single greatest American investment beyond her own borders up until that time, the Marshall Plan helped set the tone for the rest of the Cold War – that of spending to victory. It also created an expectation of America in the minds of other countries: that it would assist those looking to avoid communist domination. This expectation was not always lived up to (see Hungary and Czechoslovakia). Despite the offer of Marshall Aid being open to *any* country – including the USSR – those countries under the Soviet 'umbrella' were largely forbidden by the Kremlin to access it. The Plan succeeded in most of its aims: Europe saw the greatest economic growth in its history, communism receded in countries that became stable and prosperous, and NATO was largely built upon the foundation laid by it.

HISTORIOGRAPHY

"…it was American policies as much as (and perhaps more than) Soviet actions that finally led to the division of Europe and thus to the Cold War itself."

Michael Cox and Caroline Kennedy-Pipe
The Tragedy of American Diplomacy? Rethinking the Marshall Plan

WHERE TO FIND OUT MORE

The Marshall Plan Mystique
David Ekbladh

Marshall Plan ep. 3 The Cold War
CNN documentary series

bit.ly/2DMthvO

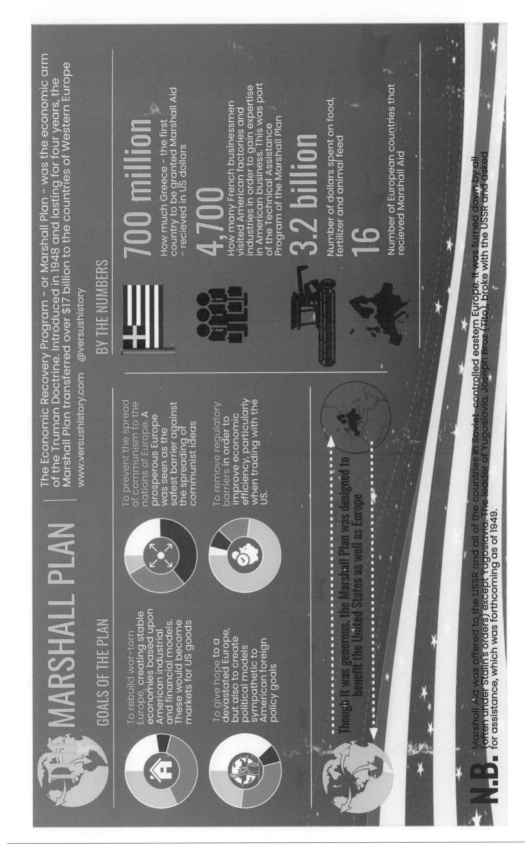

MARSHALL PLAN

The Economic Recovery Program – or Marshall Plan – was the economic arm of the Truman Doctrine. Introduced in 1948 and lasting for four years, the Marshall Plan transferred over $17 billion to the countries of Western Europe

www.versushistory.com   @versushistory

GOALS OF THE PLAN

To rebuild war-torn Europe, creating stable economies based upon American industrial and financial models. These would become markets for US goods

To give hope to a devastated Europe, but also to create political models sympathetic to American foreign policy goals

To prevent the spread of communism to the nations of Europe. A prosperous Europe was seen as the safest barrier against the spreading of communist ideas

To remove regulatory barriers in order to improve economic efficiency, particularly when trading with the US.

Though it was generous, the Marshall Plan was designed to benefit the United States as well as Europe

BY THE NUMBERS

700 million
How much Greece – the first country to be granted Marshall Aid – recieved in US dollars

4,700
How many French businessmen visited American factories and industries in order to gain expertise in American business. This was part of the Technical Assistance Program of the Marshall Plan

3.2 billion
Number of dollars spent on food, fertilizer and animal feed

16
Number of European countries that recieved Marshall Aid

N.B. Marshall Aid was offered to the USSR and all of the countries in Soviet-controlled eastern Europe. It was turned down by all (often under Stalin's orders) except Yugoslavia. The leader of Yugoslavia, Joseph Broz (Tito), broke with the USSR and asked for assistance, which was forthcoming as of 1949.

MONEY TALKS

OVERVIEW

Emerging from World War Two as by far the wealthiest country on Earth, the United States found itself in the position – and with the desire – to wield that wealth to its advantage. In the nascent Cold War, American wealth gave it the immediate edge over countries that had suffered immensely during the war – particularly the USSR. The term 'dollar imperialism' was coined by the Soviet Foreign Minister, Vyacheslav Molotov, in reference to the Marshall Plan – which he saw as a tool used by the United States to imprint its influence over Western Europe, as well as to contain the spread of communism. The US spent over $17 billion (c.202 billion in 2019 dollars) on Marshall Aid, but this does not represent the limits of American spending and investment around the globe during the Cold War – that figure is practically impossible to calculate.

SIGNIFICANCE

If we accept, as many historians do, that the Marshall Plan represented the beginning 'proper' of the Cold War, then we must also accept that so-called 'dollar imperialism' should be considered one of the Cold War's key triggers. American dollars helped to rebuild those countries of Europe who accepted Marshall Aid and, in this sense, any appraisal of US policy must consider the generosity involved. However, 'dollar imperialism', as the name suggests, was (and still is) geopolitical, self-serving, and propagandist in nature. By spending nearly 5% of their annual GDP on Marshall Aid – and much more outside of the Plan's parameters – the US were looking to accomplish exactly what the Soviets accused them of: economic, political, geostrategic, and military hegemony in Europe first, and later the world. By accepting American assistance a country was, to varying degrees, also subscribing to American global leadership – in all of its forms. For their part, the Soviets had their own attempts with 'ruble imperialism' through such things as COMECON.

HISTORIOGRAPHY

"Constituting itself at a time when decolonisation was well under way and other empires were disintegrating, US imperialism could never openly speak its name. Initially, it disguised itself as the defender of democracy against communism…"

Rohini Hensman and Marinella Correggia
US Dollar Hegemony: The Soft Underbelly of Empire

WHERE TO FIND OUT MORE

The Sword and the Dollar: Imperialism, Revolution, and the Arms Race
Michael Parenti

The Marshall Plan: Dawn of the Cold War
Ben Steil

bit.ly/3fH5ZZ

Financing a Cold War Empire
'Dollar Imperiali$m'

Term coined by Soviet Foreign Minister, Vyacheslav Molotov

"...our help should be primarily through economic and financial aid..."

President Truman

MEANING

Term meant to imply that the Marshall Plan was nothing more than a ploy by the Americans to use their economic superiority in the Cold War to create an American empire against the USSR

MONEY

$17 billion was offered to the countries of Europe under the Marshall Plan to help them recover after World War Two

BAGGAGE

The Soviet Union correctly understood that the money offered under the Marshall Plan came with 'baggage'. Any country accepting US money would have to conform to their political and economic models

IMAGE

The US knew how Marshall Aid looked to the Soviets, which is why it was also offered to the USSR and the countries of Eastern Europe

REJECTION

The USSR rejected Marshall Aid and forbade countries under its control to accept any as this would obviously undermine Soviet communist authority

CORRECT

In a sense, Molotov was right - Marshall Aid was a tool to build an American empire against the spread of Soviet communist influence. Of course, it was much more than mere 'dollar imperialism'

www.versushistory.com
@versushistory

ANYTHING YOU CAN DO...

OVERVIEW

When the US announced the Marshall Plan in 1947 it became clear almost immediately that, although it was available to all countries of Europe, any currently existing within the Soviet sphere of influence would be forbidden by Moscow from accessing it. Since the ultimate goal of the Marshall Plan was to create a political and economic hegemony over the war-shattered countries of Western Europe, the USSR made the decision to attempt something similar in the East. Proposed by the Soviet Foreign Minister, Vyacheslav Molotov, the Molotov Plan – later known as COMECON (Council of Mutual Economic Assistance) – was a series of bilateral trade agreements between its seven original member countries. Although the program was devised *before* the Marshall Plan, Molotov's version was fabricated specifically as an alternative to it, so as to present a unified economic and ideological bloc of countries that could resist American encroachment.

SIGNIFICANCE

Measured by its own objectives, the Molotov Plan must be considered a success of some significance. As socialist economies removed trade barriers, establishing in the process a form of continental econo-political cooperation, the Plan represented the first example of 'international communist integration'. Economic historians generally agree that the Plan was a key factor that helped contribute to notable economic growth of the war-ravaged countries of Eastern Europe. Of course, there was a glaring contradiction inherent in the Molotov Plan: its stated purpose was to rebuild the economies of Eastern Europe, yet the Soviet Union saw those very same economies as serving the 'mother country'. In short, the USSR exploited the resources of those countries whilst simultaneously attempting to rebuild their economies along socialist lines. If NATO and the Warsaw Pact helped divide the world militarily, then the Marshall and Molotov Plans helped divide it economically.

HISTORIOGRAPHY

"It is therefore clear that the USSR's answer to the Marshall Plan was the expansion of its own Molotov Plan to bind the satellites to each other and to strengthen their economic ties to the model state in the East (Russia)."

Morroe Berger
How the Molotov Plan Works

WHERE TO FIND OUT MORE

Moscow and the Marshall Plan: Politics, Ideology and the Onset of the Cold War, 1947
Geoffrey Roberts

Molotov Remembers: Inside Kremlin Politics
Vyacheslav Mikhailovich Molotov and Felix Chuev

bit.ly/31wBwEt

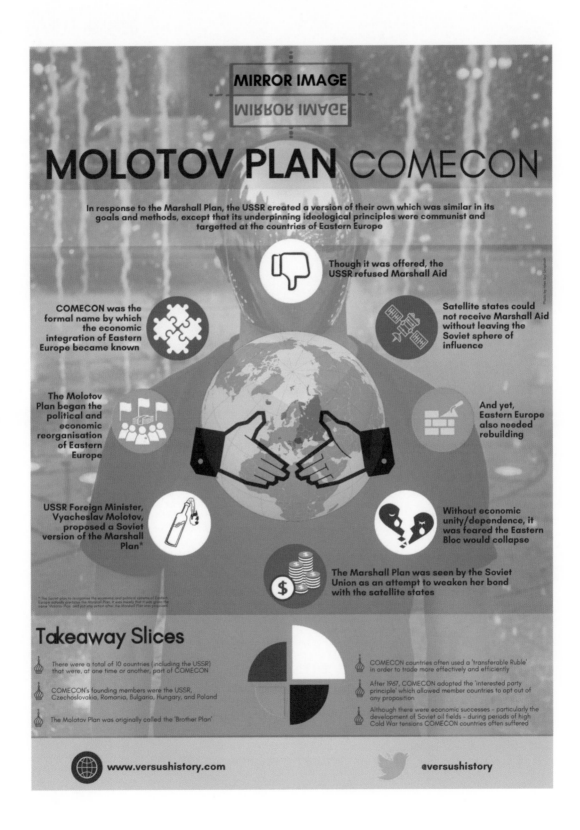

MIRROR IMAGE

MOLOTOV PLAN COMECON

In response to the Marshall Plan, the USSR created a version of their own which was similar in its goals and methods, except that its underpinning ideological principles were communist and targetted at the countries of Eastern Europe

Though it was offered, the USSR refused Marshall Aid

COMECON was the formal name by which the economic integration of Eastern Europe became known

Satellite states could not receive Marshall Aid without leaving the Soviet sphere of influence

The Molotov Plan began the political and economic reorganisation of Eastern Europe

And yet, Eastern Europe also needed rebuilding

USSR Foreign Minister, Vyacheslav Molotov, proposed a Soviet version of the Marshall Plan*

Without economic unity/dependence, it was feared the Eastern Bloc would collapse

The Marshall Plan was seen by the Soviet Union as an attempt to weaken her bond with the satellite states

* The Soviet plan to reorganise the economic and political systems of Eastern Europe actually predates the Marshall Plan. It was merely that it was given the name 'Molotov Plan' and put into action after the Marshall Plan was proposed.

Takeaway Slices

There were a total of 10 countries (including the USSR) that were, at one time or another, part of COMECON

COMECON's founding members were the USSR, Czechoslovakia, Romania, Bulgaria, Hungary, and Poland

The Molotov Plan was originally called the 'Brother Plan'

COMECON countries often used a 'transferable Ruble' in order to trade more effectively and efficiently

After 1967, COMECON adopted the 'interested party principle' which allowed member countries to opt out of any proposition

Although there were economic successes – particularly the development of Soviet oil fields – during periods of high Cold War tensions COMECON countries often suffered

www.versushistory.com

@versushistory

BUILDING BLOCKS

OVERVIEW

When the Cold War emerged from the ashes of World War Two, Germany – and Berlin in particular – became something of a literal and metaphorical epicentre for the tension, paranoia, and strategising that characterised the Cold War. Consequently, Berlin also became – as one might imagine – a natural location for Cold War 'flashpoints' between the superpowers. Sparked by the US and British unification of their zones of occupation in the West and the introduction of a West German currency – the Deutschmark – the Berlin Blockade was imposed by Stalin in an attempt to, ultimately, force the Allies out of West Berlin. Lasting from June 1948 to May 1949, the closure of all rail, road and canal access to the Allied-administered western zones of Berlin became the first true 'flashpoint' of the Cold War and almost starved and froze to death the population of West Germany.

SIGNIFICANCE

The blockade's significance is deeply embedded in the mythology of the early Cold War, being, as it was, the first major 'flashpoint' between the two superpowers. It is also notable that it resulted in the Berlin Airlift, which ultimately handed Stalin and the USSR their first real loss in the still-emerging Cold War. Stalin's removal of the blockade a year later represented a significant 'climbdown' for a leader that was looking to push the Allies out of West Berlin. Instead, it appeared to many who had the inclination to view it as such, as a brutish and miserable failure. The propaganda value of the blockade was incalculable: if ever there was a stark reminder of the differences between the West and the East, it was here: the desperate act of a totalitarian bully looking to starve West Berlin into submission, countered by the egalitarianism of a collective looking to save the lives of others. Of course, this victory for the Allies was as much one of geopolitics as it was a demonstration of genuine humanity. Nevertheless, the blockade and subsequent airlift so hardened the Cold War battle lines that not until the collapse of the Soviet Union would those lines disappear.

HISTORIOGRAPHY

"...the blockade appears more as one step in a long political struggle between two power blocs for influence than the pre-meditated act of a master criminal."

Daniel F. Harrington
The Berlin Blockade Revisited (The International History Review, Vol. 6, No. 1)

WHERE TO FIND OUT MORE

The Berlin Blockade - archive, 1948
The Guardian Online, Compiled by Richard Nelsson (bit.ly/3f6NJVP)

bit.ly/31gzJ6c

The Berlin Blockade
Ann & John Tulsa

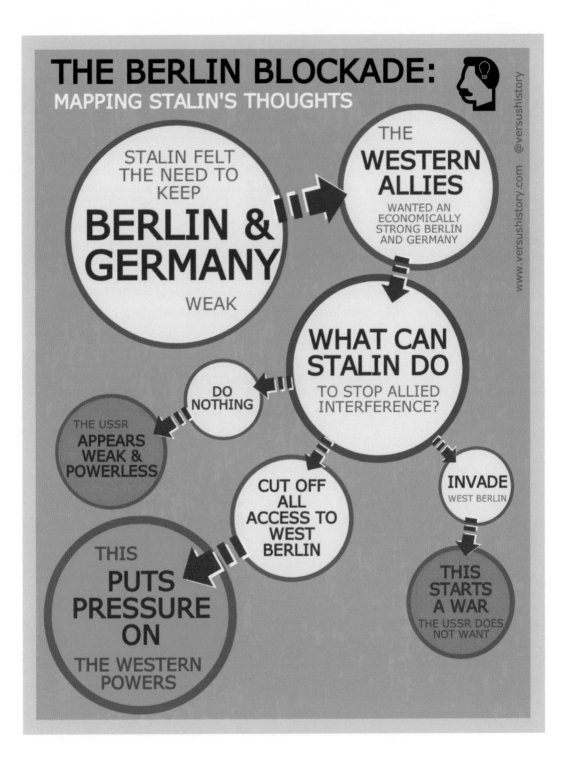

FLYING IN THE FACE OF STALIN

OVERVIEW

On June 26, 1948, 32 American C-47 planes landed in West Berlin carrying just under 90 tonnes of essential supplies to feed a population which had been blockaded by the Soviet Union. By the beginning of September, 'Operation Vittles' had become an efficient enterprise, delivering 4,500 tonnes daily via two West Berlin airports, Tempelhof and Gatow, with the construction of a third, Tegel, underway. For eleven months, three air corridors and runways became the lifeline of West Berlin's two million residents, supplying food, fuel, clothing, and construction materials. Although the blockade ended on 12 May 1948, the airlift continued until September, building up supplies to guard against further Soviet blockades.

SIGNIFICANCE

Beyond the obvious of keeping Berlin residents alive, the airlift was significant for the Cold War in two ways. Firstly, it was a concrete demonstration of the lengths to which the US and UK would go – and the resources they were prepared to invest – to achieve their goal of containing communism. This commitment was cemented during the last months of the airlift by the creation of NATO, which established a mutual defence program for much of Western Europe. Secondly, the airlift formalised the split between east and west in Germany. By the end of 1949 American, British and French-controlled areas had merged into the Federal Republic of Germany, while the German Democratic Republic was created in the East. German reunification, while still an ambition for many, felt an unlikely prospect.

HISTORIOGRAPHY

"The airlift made it possible to identify with a wider world. Berliners came to see themselves as partners with the Western powers personified by leaders (of the airlift) such as Clay, Robertson and Howley and by the pilots participating in the airlift."

Daniel F. Harrington
Berlin on the Brink: The Blockade, the Airlift and the Early Cold War

WHERE TO FIND OUT MORE

The Berlin Airlift: The Relief Operation that defined the Cold War
Barry Turner

Berlin in the Cold War: The Divided City
Thomas Flemming

bit.ly/3kCijtM

THE BERLIN AIRLIFT

ELEVEN MONTHS ON THE EDGE

aversushistory

www.versushistory.com

Brandenburg Gate Photo: Claudio Schwarz

8,000 tons of supplies carried per day (by the end)

EVERY 60 seconds on average an Allied flight landed in Berlin

68,000 people flown OUT of Berlin

2.3 million tons of cargo carried by the Allies

2,300 daily calories each W. Berliner received

277,804 total flights

THREE AIRPORTS IN WEST BERLIN USED BY THE ALLIES:

- Tempelhof (American Zone)
- Gatow (British Zone)
- Tegel (French Sector)

SAFETY IN NUMBERS

OVERVIEW

As the Cold War moved from its infant stage into its toddler stage, it naturally began to grow teeth. Once the battle lines had been drawn on either side of the 'Iron Curtain', it became clear that soldiers and weapons would be needed to defend these battle lines. Consequently, a move was made by the countries of Western Europe and North America to galvanise their respective militaries against the potential threat posed by the USSR. This move was made on April 4, 1949, when the North Atlantic Treaty was signed by twelve countries, ranging from Canada and the US to Denmark and the UK. With its HQ in Brussels, NATO was based upon the system of *collective security* (set out in Article 5 of the Treaty), which would view an attack on one of its members as an attack on all.

SIGNIFICANCE

Since NATO was patently created as a military deterrent against a potential Soviet military attack on its members in the West, it rather inevitably led to a similar alliance being created in the East. In 1955, after West Germany was permitted membership of NATO, the Soviet Union established the Warsaw Pact, arguably the most significant consequence of which was that the Cold War was now militarised. Alone, this development is sufficient to demonstrate NATO's profound impact on the Cold War. Naturally, NATO also became one of the key elements of the US policy of containment – made more obvious by the appointment of its first Supreme Allied Commander: General Dwight D. Eisenhower. In the first twenty years of its existence, NATO spent more than $3 billion on developing its military 'infrastructure' – at least a third of which was financed by, and procured from, the United States. As one would imagine, this led, unsurprisingly, to American military presences in much of Western Europe. NATO also signalled, once and for all, that the Grand Alliance was dead.

HISTORIOGRAPHY

"Yet, behind this…alliance structure you see that… it is a bilateral system, with particular countries on the one hand and the United States on the other…(there is a) great scramble before the door of the American Treasury to see who is first in line for the hand-out."

Edgar S. Furniss Jr.
Problems Facing NATO

WHERE TO FIND OUT MORE

NATO at 70: A Historiographical Approach
Linda Risso (Editor)

A Short History of NATO
https://www.nato.int/cps/en/natohq/declassified_139339.htm

bit.ly/2DIDc2Na

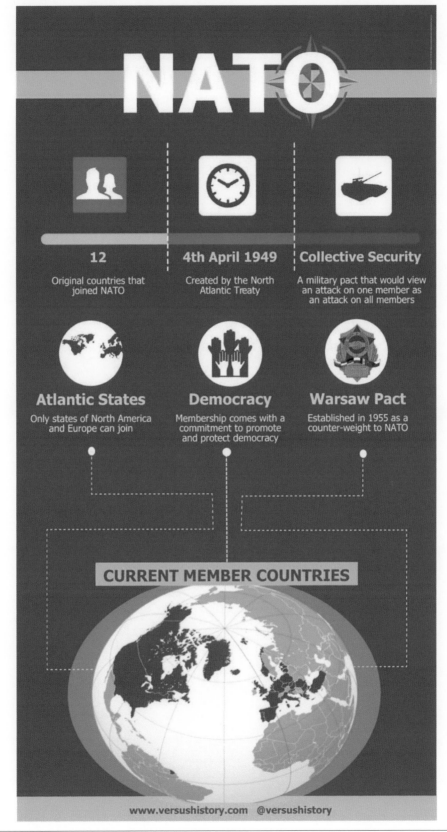

NATO

12

Original countries that joined NATO

4th April 1949

Created by the North Atlantic Treaty

Collective Security

A military pact that would view an attack on one member as an attack on all members

Atlantic States

Only states of North America and Europe can join

Democracy

Membership comes with a commitment to promote and protect democracy

Warsaw Pact

Established in 1955 as a counter-weight to NATO

CURRENT MEMBER COUNTRIES

www.versushistory.com   @versushistory

DIVIDING LINES

OVERVIEW

Less than five years after the end of World War Two, America was once again at war in the East. This time it was as part of a United Nations 'police action' in the Korean peninsula. The final phase of World War Two in the Pacific saw the Allies – America and the USSR – pushing Japan out of Korea. The Russians had done so from the north and the Americans from the south. It was agreed that, until Korea was sufficiently stable and Japanese surrender complete, the two powers would administer the peninsula separately. To do so, they 'temporarily' divided Korea in two – along the 38th line of latitude – with the ultimate aim of reunification through free elections. It quickly became clear that this aim was potentially dangerous to the ambitions of both superpowers. Consequently, when the Soviet-backed North, under the leadership of Kim Il-sung, invaded the US-backed South, under Syngman Rhee, in June 1950, it was near-inevitable that the two superpowers would be involved.

SIGNIFICANCE

Perhaps the greatest impact of the Korean War on the development of the Cold War is that it was the first 'proxy war' engaged in by the superpowers. Since the Cold War could not devolve into direct fighting between the USSR and US because of the potential for nuclear war, both sides needed to develop other means of 'winning'. Consequently, the Korean War created a precedent for how the Cold War might be fought and won; it also resulted in something of a blueprint for how proxy wars might be conducted. In addition, it can also be viewed as laying the groundwork for future interventions in Asia. Despite the US fighting under the flag of the UN, this was very much an American intercession: 90% of the military equipment and personnel given over to the mission was from the US. As a result, one could argue that the war was fought as part of the US policy of containment – only this time it was in Asia.

HISTORIOGRAPHY

"Korea established a pattern... followed in American wars in Vietnam, Iraq, and Afghanistan... wars without declaration and without the political consensus and the resolve to meet specific and changing goals. They are improvisational wars. They are dangerous."

James Wright
What We Learned from the Korean War

WHERE TO FIND OUT MORE

The Coldest Winter: America and the Korean War
David Halberstam

Brothers at War – The Unending Conflict in Korea
Sheila Miyoshi Jager

bit.ly/30sVgJB

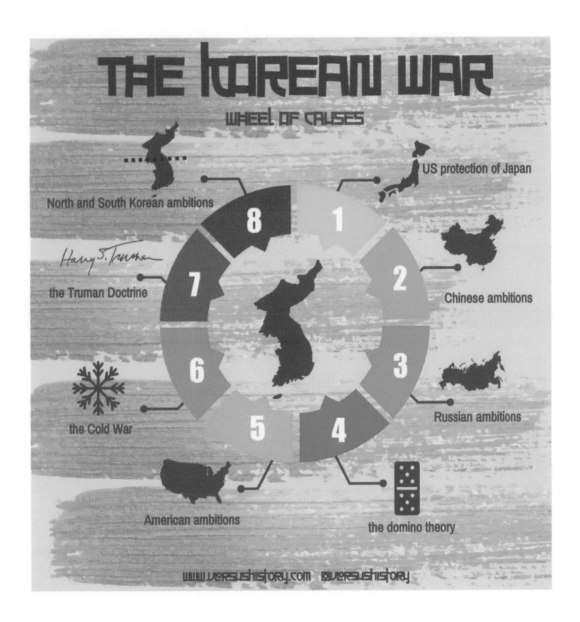

A STAGED WAR

OVERVIEW

Beginning in June 1950 with the invasion of the South by the North, the Korean War represented the first US military incursion into Asia since World War Two. Despite the American response to the invasion being as part of a UN 'police action', it was very much a US-led undertaking. General Douglas MacArthur took command of UN forces and helped shape the war strategy which involved, to begin with, the pushing of North Korean forces out of South Korea and back to the 38th parallel. Once this was achieved, MacArthur took the decision to alter the initial plan of containment and embark on one that involved 'rolling back' communism to the Chinese border. Warned by Mao that doing so would bring a military response from the Chinese, MacArthur pressed on. Despite Truman's concerns, UN forces crossed the 38th parallel and began, with initial success, rolling North Korean forces back. When they crossed the Yalu River, a quarter of a million Chinese soldiers poured into North Korea, pushing UN forces back below the 38th parallel. Labelled as insubordinate, MacArthur was removed by Truman. Eventually, the UN forces were able to push the forces of the North back to the 38th parallel, where they remain to this day.

SIGNIFICANCE

Very few, if any, events in history can be neatly sliced into perfect temporal portions with clear, unfettered beginnings and ends. To claim that something as complex as war can or should be divided into 'hermetically sealed' time stages, one entirely separate from the next, undermines the intractable web of causality enmeshed within every event, no matter how big or small. Every temporal moment inevitably transitions into the next, and the next and the next, with barely an 'adieu' to time gone by, or a 'hello' to the one arriving. Consequently, by presenting the Korean War as a staged conflict one inevitably runs the risk of simplifying history, and yet, and yet…that is the point of this book – to make complex histories easier to study.

HISTORIOGRAPHY

"…most scholars… agreed that by pursuing the retreating North Korean Army across the 38th parallel…the Americans needlessly provoked the Chinese into intervening."

Kathryn Weathersby
The Korean War Revisited

WHERE TO FIND OUT MORE

A Substitute for Victory
Rosemary Foot

The Korean War
Max Hastings

bit.ly/3kbYJUN

WWW.VERSUSHISTORY.COM @VERSUSHISTORY

6
STAGES OF THE
KOREAN WAR

A civil war. A proxy war. A UN 'police action'.

1
the postwar division of Korea

After the US & USSR defeated Japan, they decided to divide Korea 'temporarily' along the 38th parallel

2
the north invades the south

On 25th June, 1950 90,000 North Korean soldiers invade the south and get all the way to Pusan

3
with UN help the south pushes back

In September, UN forces (mostly US soldiers) under General MacArthur push the North Koreans back to the 38th parallel

4
the abandonment of containment

MacArthur & Truman make the decision to cross the 38th parallel and reunify Korea, risking Chinese involvement

5
China sends in the troops

350,000 Chinese troops cross the Yalu river and help push UN forces back below the 38th parallel. The gamble had failed

6
back to the 38th parallel

By June 1951, massive casualties on both sides led to discussions of an armistice, which was signed 27th July, 1953

CASTING A SPELL ON AMERICA

OVERVIEW

Outside of those who had, at one time or another, occupied the office of the presidency, Joseph McCarthy – the junior Senator for Wisconsin – became, albeit fleetingly, perhaps the most influential US politician of the twentieth century. Just as the Cold War was generating fear across the world, McCarthy saw an opportunity to raise his own political profile by announcing in 1950, on what would have been the 140th birthday of Abraham Lincoln, that he had "…here in my hand a list of 205 (State Department Employees)… known… as being members of the Communist Party". For the next five years, McCarthyism – a term coined by Herbert Block, a cartoonist for the Washington Post – swept America, destroying the lives of innocent people with the mere accusation of communist sympathies.

SIGNIFICANCE

The hysteria generated by the early Cold War context and utilised so effectively by McCarthy – in televised congressional hearings, newspaper columns, radio interviews and books – created such an indelible trauma in American life that a noun was created in his dubious honour: *McCarthyism*. With the confluence of the Berlin Blockade, the 'fall' of China, the Soviet detonation of an atomic bomb, and the Korean War, tension in the Cold War was high. As espionage on both sides of the iron curtain became a tool-of-the-trade, the possibility that spies were undermining the American government became a threat – both real and imaginary. McCarthyism came to be symbolic of, and a contributor to, the anti-communist frenzy within American political discourse that sought out the imaginary at the expense of the real. So impactful were McCarthy's 'witch-hunts' that even presidents would come to shrink at the very implication that they were 'soft' on communism. In addition, hundreds of innocent lives were destroyed by McCarthy's 'loyalty review boards' that trampled gleefully and with malice over their constitutional rights.

HISTORIOGRAPHY

"It is the use of the big lie and the unfounded accusation against any citizen in the name of Americanism or security. It is the rise to power of the demagogue who lives on untruth; it is the spreading of fear and the destruction of faith."

Former President, Harry S. Truman

WHERE TO FIND OUT MORE

Cold War, Cool Medium: Television, McCarthyism, and American Culture
Thomas Doherty

Many are the Crimes: McCarthyism in America
Ellen Schrecker

bit.ly/2Xve9dj

THE WARSAW PACT: A REFLECTION

OVERVIEW

When, on May 9, 1955, West Germany joined NATO, it became abundantly clear to the Soviet Union that not only would Germany *not* be reuniting any time soon, but also that a new existential threat to their hegemony over eastern Europe had emerged: a rearmed West Germany. As an almost immediate response (though, to be fair, one that had its origins in the time before NATO) the USSR and seven other European countries established the Warsaw Pact. The Pact functioned, by-and-large, in the same manner as NATO, with *collective security* as its founding principle. In many respects it was a mirror image of NATO: a rearmed East Germany was created as a counterweight to West Germany, inclusion in the Pact helped consolidate Russian political/ideological control over their sphere of influence, and it helped contain the spread of western influence.

SIGNIFICANCE

Although it may seem as such, the Warsaw Pact was not simply a knee-jerk reaction to NATO or the remilitarising of West Germany, in fact the USSR actually petitioned for membership of NATO in 1954. Though the Pact was rushed into existence once West Germany joined NATO, the fear of a rearmed West Germany had been present amongst many of the countries of Eastern Europe (not to mention France) since the end of the war. The Pact formalised (albeit hastily) a long-held desire for a defensive military bloc against a resurgent Federal Republic of Germany. Of course, it also reaffirmed Soviet control over its satellite states. Alongside NATO, the Warsaw Pact served to militarise the Cold War, ultimately raising the stakes in every potential flashpoint. Having said this, the two military blocs never directly waged war on each other, primarily because of the dire consequences of such a conflagration. Instead, both blocs exerted their influence in proxy wars, all the while containing the movements of one another through geostrategic manoeuvres and deterrence.

HISTORIOGRAPHY

"The concept of a separate communist alliance had already been conceived at the "European" Security Conference in November 1954. Although the foundation of the Warsaw Pact was 'thoroughly orchestrated' by the Soviet Union, the idea… was, in fact, a Polish one, which is why the alliance was founded in Warsaw."

Laura Carolien Crump
The Warsaw Pact Reconsidered

WHERE TO FIND OUT MORE

Warsaw Pact Intervention in the Third World: Aid and Influence in the Cold War
Philip E. Muehlenbeck and Natalia Telepneva (eds.)

NATO and the Warsaw Pact: Intrabloc Conflicts
Mary Ann Heiss and S. Victor Papacosma (eds.)

bit.ly/31jfgOJ

MILITARISING THE COLD WAR

www.versushistory.com   @versushistory

Balancing the scales with the....

WARSAW PACT

Established in 1955, the Warsaw Pact was the military complement to COMECON

Why was it formed?

Remember:

Established in

1955

Khrushchev was the Soviet leader at the time

Eisenhower was the American leader at the time

NATO
As a military counterweight to the newly formed NATO

SATELLITE STATES
To help maintain control over the countries of Eastern Europe

COMMUNISM
To protect communist systems established in Eastern Europe

COLLECTIVE SECURITY
It would act as a deterrent to western military confrontation

www.versushistory.com   @versushistory

BANDUNG TOGETHER

OVERVIEW

In 1955, 29 African and Asian countries met at the Bandung Conference in Indonesia. Many of these countries were newly formed, having gained independence from European empires. Independence, territorial integrity, and neutrality were at the heart of the declaration agreed by the conference. This group of nations, later joined by many others – particularly from the Caribbean and Latin America – came to be formalised in 1961 as the Non-Aligned Movement (NAM) which would form the third, often ignored power bloc of the Cold War.

SIGNIFICANCE

The NAM's genesis came from recognising the vulnerability of individual countries to exploitation and unwanted intervention in the 'great game' being played out by the superpowers. In this sense the NAM was significant, as it gave many nascent nations greater security. So too, by operating as a voting bloc within the United Nations General Assembly, did smaller nations gain a greater degree of influence which could not be ignored; one that meant both superpowers often felt a need to court them. The NAM's avowed neutrality did not, however, mean ambivalence. Key figures such as Nasser, Tito and Castro were outspoken, indeed their position as leading figures of the NAM gave them a vehicle and platform from which to project international influence, arguably forcing the superpowers to be more cautious in their dealings with the developing world.

HISTORIOGRAPHY

"To declare the end of colonialism and to conjure Afro-Asian solidarity was a significant symbolic act...but this declaration (at Bandung) could not in itself...gloss over the fundamentally diverging interests of these new states. Regional conflicts had a profound impact on the way Asian, Middle Eastern and African states reacted to the manoeuvres of the Great Powers."

N. Miskovic, H Fischer-Tine, N. Boskovska (eds.)
The Non-Aligned Movement and the Cold War: Delhi - Bandung – Belgrade

WHERE TO FIND OUT MORE

The Non-Aligned Movement: Genesis, Organization and Politics
Jürgen Dinkel

The Cold War in the Third World
Robert J. McMahon

bit.ly/30sA3Q5

SHOPPING FOR ALLIES

THE NON-ALIGNED MOVEMENT

KEY MOMENTS IN THE MOVEMENT

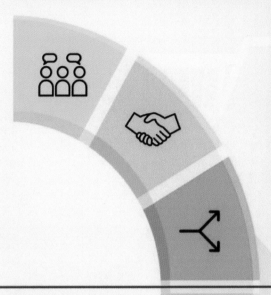

April 1955
Bandung Conference

Exploratory meeting of 29 Afro-Asian nations focusses on economic cooperation and declares neutrality in the Cold War

September 1961
Belgrade Conference

First official meeting establishes the NAM: 25 countries including India, Sri Lanka, Yugoslavia and Egypt

December 1979
Soviet Invasion of Afghanistan

Divisions over the invasion, and members such as Cuba's refusal to condemn the USSR's actions led to a splintering of the bloc's cohesion

IDEALS OF THE NAM EXPRESSED IN 1961

NEUTRALITY

"The existing military blocs...necessarily provoke periodical aggravations of international relations."

ANTI-COLONIALISM

"All natons have the right of unity, self-determinaton, and independence."

DISARMAMENT

"Disarmament is an imperative need and the most urgent task of mankind."

THE SCALE OF THE NAM TODAY

2/3 of UN members
55% of the world's population

GUNNING FOR VICTORY

OVERVIEW

Initiated by the dropping of atomic bombs on Hiroshima and Nagasaki, the arms race was a constant throughout the Cold War. The struggle for technological superiority required huge investment in weaponry, both nuclear and conventional, a phenomenon that would cause significant domestic criticism for both superpowers at different times in their Cold War histories. From the mid–1950s, the arms race took on its best-known character, spreading into space and dominated by the notion of mutually assured destruction. It was the decline of this 'balance of terror' through American technological dominance, both real and perceived, as well as the crumbling Soviet economy, that brought an end to the arms race by 1991.

SIGNIFICANCE

Leadership in the arms race was, in the eyes of many, synonymous with being on top in the Cold War as a whole. Similarly, feelings of inferiority, such as the perceived bomber and missile 'gaps' the USA feared in the 1950s, provoked deep fears and existential questions for governments on both sides, highlighting the critical importance of the arms race. Such feelings and questions, by virtue of the arms race's nuclear nature, were felt globally by civilian populations living with the near-constant fear of imminent apocalypse. Ironically, it was the very cataclysmic destructive power created by the arms race that also helped develop a consensus that, other than being a deterrent, it was a senseless waste of resources.

HISTORIOGRAPHY

"The most important reason why the Cold War affected everyone in the world was the threat of nuclear destruction that it implied...there is no doubt that the nuclear arms race was profoundly dangerous."

Odd Arne Westad
The Cold War: A World History

WHERE TO FIND OUT MORE

The Bomb: Presidents, Generals and the Secret History of Nuclear War
Fred Kaplan

Arms Races in International Politics: From the Nineteenth to the Twenty-First Century
Thomas Mahnken, Joseph Maiolo and David Stevenson (eds.)

bit.ly/3inRXtF

THE ARMS RACE

www.versushistory.com @versushistory

By **1953** arms spending had accelerated, reaching $49.6bn in the USA

To put this into perspective, this is almost double the USSR's $25.5bn & quadruple what the USA spent in 1949

The arms race was an ongoing struggle that lasted throughout the whole of the Cold War

In **1949** the USSR successfully tested their first atomic bomb bringing an end to the US nuclear monopoly

Kickstarted by the dropping of the first atomic bomb on Hiroshima

6th August 1945

Détente helped bring about the first freeze of some nuclear weapons in

1972

S

with the SALT I agreements

1983 saw the announcement of 'Star Wars' by Ronald Reagan

The anticipated cost of the USSR keeping up with such developments helped bring about the end of the arms race

The high tech weapons developed in the arms race were coupled with significant conventional forces

The US army consisted of **2-3.5 million** troops, while the USSR's fluctuated between **4 & 5 million**

The arms race gave rise to a huge number of acronyms to describe the weapons, technologies, conferences and strategies

NUTS   SDI

START   MIRV

ICBM   MAD   SLBM

INF   SALT   ABM

The **INF** Treaty was the first agreement signed to reduce nuclear weapons, eliminating those with a range of 300-3400 miles

---

The arms race was dominated by new technologies

1952

First successful test of a Hydrogen bomb

1955

First submarine-launched ballistic missile

1957

First intercontinental ballistic missile

1968

First MIRV, with multiple warheads on one missile

HUNGARY FOR CHANGE

OVERVIEW

On October 23, 1956, some 20,000 protestors took to the streets of Budapest. Calling for major reforms including the removal of Soviet troops, free elections, and a free press, they also tore down a statue of Stalin. The previous few years had seen such feelings reach fever pitch in Hungary. Serious economic decline, 'musical chairs' at the top of the Hungarian Communist Party and orchestrated by Moscow, coupled to a seeming new dawn ushered in by Khrushchev's de-Stalinisation, had encouraged Hungarians to take to the streets. Over the next 10 days there were frantic attempts to bring order: Soviet troops were deployed and the Prime Ministership was passed like a hot potato from person to person. One of those who took on the role of PM – Imre Nagy – proposed a series of reforms. Ultimately, however, the different, competing demands of protestors, the Hungarian communist elite and the USSR, could not be reconciled and on November 4 the USSR launched a full-scale invasion of Hungary.

SIGNIFICANCE

The crushing of the Hungarian Revolution sent a firm message: the USSR was ready and willing to use force to ensure it retained control over a strictly communist Eastern Europe, with the Daily Mail dubbing events "The Murder of Hungary". There was increased hardship in Hungary as a result. Despite being outgunned, rebels fought against the Soviet invasion sporadically until the middle of 1957, suffering some 20,000 casualties, while hundreds of thousands were displaced. On a geopolitical level, however, events in Hungary were to have little impact. In effect they reinforced the existing status quo, while other events, such as the Suez Crisis, the beginning of the Space Race and unfolding events in Cuba, threatened to upend the existing world order.

HISTORIOGRAPHY

"The world's attention was riveted on the uprising in Budapest...The editors of Time magazine jettisoned their candidates for "Man of the Year" at the last minute to put a painting of a composite "Hungarian Freedom Fighter" on the cover as "Man of the Year". But in less than a year, the Revolution was overshadowed by Sputnik"

John P. C. Matthews
Explosion: The Hungarian Revolution of 1956

WHERE TO FIND OUT MORE

Twelve Days: Revolution 1956. How the Hungarians Tried to Topple their Soviet Masters
Victor Sebestyen

Blood and Sand: Suez, Hungary and the Crisis that Shook the World
Alex von Tunzelmann

bit.ly/3gKjQLR

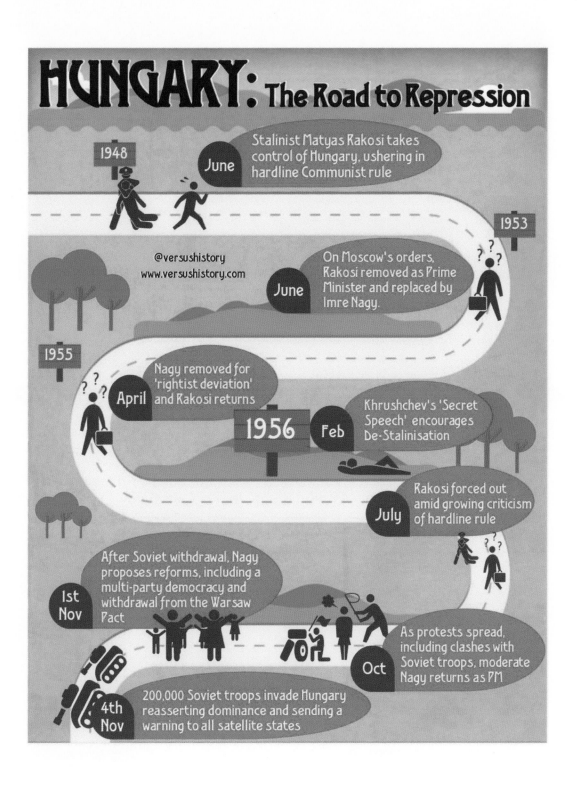

(IN)FIDEL

OVERVIEW

In the early hours of New Year's Day 1959, the President of Cuba, Fulgencio Batista, fled the country on receiving news that his forces were defeated at the Battle of Santa Clara by Cuban revolutionaries. From their base in the remote Cuban mountains, these forces, led by Fidel Castro and the controversially iconic Che Guevara, had been waging a 7-year guerrilla campaign to oust the US-aligned Batista. The new government under Castro would nationalise American-owned businesses and pivot towards the USSR, rather than the USA, for support.

SIGNIFICANCE

As well as ushering in a profound structural overhaul of the Cuban economy, Castro's revolution caused a sea-change in the Cold War. Crucially, due to its impact on US-USSR relations, it provoked the Bay of Pigs invasion and the subsequent missile crisis, yet it also somewhat shifted the balance of power in the Western Hemisphere. Castro was to exhort similar revolutions in Latin America and beyond, sending military aid to insurgencies in such diverse places as Nicaragua, Angola, and Ethiopia. President Kennedy's belief that US policy had 'manufactured the Castro movement' led to attempts at changing US relations with Latin America and the introduction of the Alliance for Progress. The legacy continues to be felt in the 21st century through the continued US embargo on, and frosty relations with, Havana.

HISTORIOGRAPHY

"The Cuban Revolution was responsible not only for the revolutionary ferment that spread across Latin America. Because it posed an existential threat to Latin America's elites and US economic and geopolitical interests, that wave of revolution created a powerful wave of reaction that engulfed the region."

T. Wright
Latin America in the Era of the Cuban Revolution and Beyond

WHERE TO FIND OUT MORE

Inside the Cuban Revolution
Julia Sweig

Back Channel to Cuba: The Hidden History of Negotiations between Washington and Havana
William M. LeoGrande & Peter Kornbluh

bit.ly/33vCFii

THE CUBAN REVOLUTION

WHY WAS THERE A REVOLUTION IN CUBA, 1959?

FULGENCIO BATISTA

A brutal and corrupt dictator who ruled Cuba with an iron fist. He was very close with the American government and US businessmen.

The US supported and then recognised his military coup in 1954 which saw him take the presidency and cancel elections; this made him deeply unpopular with Cuban nationalists and ordinary Cubans alike.

20,000 Number of Cubans Batista murdered in 7 years.

FIDEL CASTRO

A socialist revolutionary nationalist who wanted to overthrow Batista and reduce the influence of America in the political and economic affairs of Cuba.

Waged a guerrilla war against Batista from his jungle camps in the Sierra Maestra mountains.

US INFLUENCE

Since their victory over the Spanish in 1898, the US maintained influence in Cuba, initially as its 'protector'. This role would grow into a greater degree of political and economic control.

www.versushistory.com

@versushistory

SOCIO-ECONOMIC PROBLEMS

- Only 10% of rural homes had electricity
- Only 15% of rural homes had running water
- Most children did not attend school
- 25% of the population was illiterate
- Over 40% of the workforce was under/unemployed
- Cuba was a one-crop economy: sugar. If the harvest failed, then the economy failed - which it did, frequently

US & THE ECONOMY

"At the beginning of 1959, United States companies owned about 40 percent of the Cuban sugar lands, almost all the cattle ranches, 90 percent of the mines and mineral concessions, 80 percent of the utilities, practically all the oil industry, and supplied two-thirds of Cuba's imports."

John F. Kennedy

THE ATTRACTION OF SOCIALISM

It is crucial to remember that, under such social, economic and political pressures, many Cubans felt that socialism/communism offered them a solution to their problems. It was believed by many that Fidel Castro's revolution was their best option.

JFK TAKES A BIG SWIG OF (S)WINE

OVERVIEW

After the Cuban Revolution of 1959, which effectively replaced a repressive American-backed regime with, what would ultimately become, a Soviet-backed communist one, American policy-makers at the highest level immediately began looking for ways and means to return the Caribbean island back into the US sphere of influence. Once JFK entered the White House, those efforts went into overdrive. A number of Cuban exiles that had fled to the US after the revolution formed the counter-revolutionary military unit called *Brigade 2506*. It had one goal: to overthrow Castro's government. With CIA training and funding, over 1400 men of Brigade 2506 launched from Guatemala and Nicaragua, landing at Playa Girón beach in the Bay of Pigs on April 17th. After initial success, the landing groups were overwhelmed by Castro's forces and compelled to surrender three days later. Once word got out to the international press, JFK walked back his commitment to the incursion and refused to provide much needed air support. The Bay of Pigs invasion was over.

SIGNIFICANCE

The failure of the Bay of Pigs invasion had a profound impact on the Cold War, JFK's presidency, and the historical trajectory of Cuba. The failure confirmed to Castro that America was actively seeking to destroy his regime. This confirmation gave him little choice but to forge an even closer alliance with the USSR – for both military and economic protection. Concurrently, it drove the final nail in the coffin of Cuba-United States relations, which had worsened since 1959 but were not yet dead before the attempted invasion. Humiliated, JFK, ever sensitive to public criticism, committed to proving himself a sterner, but more thoughtful, test for any future communist challenges. Operation Mongoose – covert plans to assassinate and overthrow Castro – began in earnest. The invasion also gave Castro a reason for inviting the USSR to place nuclear weapons in Cuba – an invitation that would lead to the Cuban Missile Crisis.

HISTORIOGRAPHY

"The consequence of the Bay of Pigs failure wasn't an acceptance of Castro and his control of Cuba but, rather, a renewed determination to bring him down by stealth."

Robert Dallek
JFK vs. the Military

WHERE TO FIND OUT MORE

The Brilliant Disaster: JFK, Castro, and America's Doomed Invasion of Cuba's Bay of Pigs
Jim Rasenberger

Bay of Pigs Declassified: The Secret CIA Report on the Invasion of Cuba
Peter Kornbluh (ed.)

bit.ly/2EK1RV

THE BAY OF PIGS INCIDENT

17TH APRIL 1961

A DEBACLE THAT DEFINED A PRESIDENCY

1 At all costs, JFK wanted US support for the invasion to be kept a secret

2 Hoping that the Cuban people would rise up in solidarity with them, 1,400 CIA-trained Cuban exiles landed at the Bay of Pigs in American-supplied boats, to overthrow Castro. These were Brigade 2506

3 Brigade 2506 immediately came under heavy fire. The Cuban airforce controlled the skies, sank escort ships, and strafed the invading soldiers

4 Castro ordered 20,000 soldiers to advance towards the beaches

5 JFK authorised a limited 'air umbrella' of air support – 6 unmarked US aircraft – which arrived late and were shot down

6 Almost 1,200 of Brigade 2506 surrendered, 100 were killed and the rest escaped to sea

The plan to overthrow Castro was devised under the previous president, Eisenhower

The CIA-backed and JFK-approved attempt to overthrow Castro's new government in Cuba was a defining moment in Kennedy's nascent presidency, as well as in the evolution of the Cold War

The 'Bay of Pigs'/Bahía de Cochinos

1,400 Cuban exiles launch Nicaragua on 17th April and 1,400 from Guatemala

www.versushistory.com

U2: PLAYING WITH THE EDGE

OVERVIEW

On May 1, 1960, US air force pilot Gary Powers made the first attempt to traverse the USSR aerially. The intention was to fly from Pakistan to Norway, photographing Soviet military targets from his U2 spy plane. Soviet attempts to intercept his plane with fighters failed due to the extreme altitude at which the U2 plane flew, officially up to 70,000 feet. However, he was shot down by surface to air missiles near modern day Yekaterinburg and, after failing to take his suicide pill, captured by the Soviets. The US initially claimed that a NASA weather plane had gone missing, however this was shown to be false when Gary Powers was paraded in front of the press and put on trial in the USSR for espionage.

SIGNIFICANCE

The U2 incident was a significant propaganda victory for the USSR and Khrushchev. By withholding Powers until the USA had concocted a story, which could then be disproved, they were able to put egg on American faces. Perhaps more importantly, the Paris Summit of May 1960, the first involving US and Soviet leaders for more than 5 years, was overshadowed by the incident and the relationship between Eisenhower and Khrushchev became increasingly acrimonious. Alongside the concurrent disagreements over Berlin, the incident was a key component in helping deepen the mistrust at the heart of US-Soviet relations, thereby creating the context for the high-stakes crises over Berlin and Cuba in the subsequent years.

HISTORIOGRAPHY

"The downing of the U2 was the CIA's first massive public failure, the first time many Americans discovered that their government practiced espionage. May 1960 was the first time many learned that their leaders did not always tell the truth."

Michael Beschloss
Mayday: Eisenhower, Khrushchev and the U2 Affair

WHERE TO FIND OUT MORE

A Brotherhood of Spies: The U2 and the CIA's Secret War
Monte Reel

Spy Flights of the Cold War
Paul Lashmar

bit.ly/2DwbzMR

www.versushistory.com @versushistory
GARY POWERS &
THE U2 SPY PLANE INCIDENT
On 1st May 1960, an American spy plane - the U2 'Dragon Lady' - flying at an altitude close to 70,000 feet was shot down over the Soviet Union. The fallout from this event raised Cold War tensions and set any chance of détente between the two superpowers back a number of years
THIS FLIGHT WAS CODENAMED: OPERATION GRAND SLAM
MISSION GOALS: PHOTOGRAPH NUCLEAR AND MILITARY SITES
THE RUSSIANS WERE EXPECTING THIS FLIGHT
THE EVENT DESTROYED THE SUBSEQUENT FOUR POWERS SUMMIT
POWERS CAPTURED BY THE RUSSIANS NEAR YEKATERINBURG
POWERS TAKES OFF FROM PESHAWAR, PAKISTAN
Photo of Powers: RIA Novosti archive, image #35174 / Chernov / CC-BY-SA 3.0 / CC BY-SA
1,300
The number of miles Powers was in to Russian territory when he was shot down
"SUDDENLY THERE WAS A DULL 'THUMP'"
NINE HOURS
The expected duration of the flight into Soviet airspace. It lasted just four and a half
10TH FEBRUARY, 1962
Powers was released by the Soviets in a prisoner exchange with the US
S-75 DVINA
The Soviet-designed, high altitude, surface-to-air missile that brought Powers down
SILVER DOLLAR
Powers was equipped with a fake silver dollar that carried a small needle and poison. He was to use this if captured. Obviously, he never did
28
The number of missions Powers had flown in the U2, including this last one
(U.S. Air Force photo/Master Sgt. Rose Reynolds)

WALL OF SHAME

OVERVIEW

Once the division of Germany was made permanent by the creation of the GDR and the FRG, it became clear that the points at which both states adjoined one another would become the areas of highest tension. These tensions were made even keener in Berlin, where the two sides not only existed in closer proximity to one another than anywhere else in the world, but also because West Berlin existed as an island in the 'sea of East Germany'. In short, the very existence of a successful West Berlin undermined every effort of the Soviet Union to present East Germany as a beacon of communist superiority; the contrast was simply too stark. As a consequence of this contrast, many millions of East Berliners, attracted by the opportunities of the West and repelled by the repression of the East, regularly defected through West Berlin to the western side of the 'Iron Curtain'. In an attempt to stem the flow of migrants moving westward and squeeze the Allies into leaving Berlin, Walter Ulbricht – the Chairman of the GDR State Council – signed an order on August 12 to build a wall around West Berlin. Building on the wall began the next day.

SIGNIFICANCE

Calling the wall the 'Antifascistischer Schutzwall', the East German government was able to immediately cut off all unauthorised crossings at the East-West Berlin border. Families and friends residing on either side of the wall were now permanently separated by a wall that grew in both height and sophistication over the years, as an almost unimaginable security apparatus was established to prevent border movement. Although the wall sent shockwaves across the Cold War world and revealed the extent to which the USSR would go in order to keep control of its peoples in Europe, the wall also had the ironic effect of defusing the tension in Berlin, as even JFK conceded, "…a wall is a hell of a lot better than a war". However, until its destruction in 1989, the Berlin Wall served as a clear reminder of the ideological, economic, and geographical differences between the West and the East.

HISTORIOGRAPHY

"Although nobody would say it publicly in the West, the Berlin Wall removed this destabilising factor from the Cold War and a collective sigh of relief was heaved since… a new refugee crisis would not become the pretext for a third World War."

Patrick Major
The Berlin Wall Crisis: The View from Below

WHERE TO FIND OUT MORE

Berlin Wall: The Night the Iron Curtain Closed (Documentary)
Ania Poullain-Majchrzak, Bill Thomas (Directors)

Chippin' Away
Song by Crosby, Stills & Nash

bit.ly/30rEsmq

THE BERLIN WALL

156 km

The length of barbed wire stockpiled by East German authorities that would then be used to encircle West Berlin

5 REASONS I BUILT THE WALL

"No one has the intention to erect a wall"

Walter Ulbricht, East Germany's chief decision-maker who, on 12th August 1961, signed the order to build the wall

The Berlin Ultimatum

In November 1958 I told the Western powers to withdraw from Berlin within six months, handing West Berlin over to us in East Germany. They refused.

The U2 Crisis

When Gary Powers is shot down over my country, the Paris Summit between Eisenhower and I is called off. The Americans cannot be trusted.

Western Espionage & Interference

West Berlin is in the heart of East Germany - which is ours - allowing the Allies to interfere in our territory. This is unacceptable and must be stopped.

The Brain Drain

Too many refugees are fleeing from East to West Berlin - causing embarrassment and a drain in skilled people. I must stop this.

Stark Economic Differences

The obvious prosperity in West Berlin is very attractive to the people under our control in East Berlin. I must stop them leaving for a better economic life.

GERMANY
BERLIN

EAST BERLIN

WEST BERLIN

BERLIN WALL

www.versushistory.com @versushistory

LUCKY NUMBER 13

OVERVIEW

For thirteen days in October 1962, the world came as close to nuclear conflict as at any point in the 'atomic age'. When, on the 14th of that month, an American U2 spy plane, flying 13 miles above Cuba, snapped photographs of Soviet missile sites in various stages of construction, it set off a chain of events which took the world to the brink of a nuclear exchange. For a brief but dangerous time, Cuba became ground zero for the Cold War 'game' of brinkmanship. Within thirteen days, the crisis was over and the world breathed a sigh of relief as Khrushchev and Kennedy negotiated away from the brink of a nuclear war they, and their respective countries, had helped move the world towards in the first place.

SIGNIFICANCE

Obviously, its nuclear *nature* is what helps bring a significance to the Cuban Missile Crisis that elevates it above many of the other Cold War clashes between the two superpowers. However, its importance goes further than this. Perhaps its greatest significance is the way it helped shape the Cold War. Once over, the USSR and US introduced elements of détente which included a direct telephone 'hotline' between Moscow and Washington, and the Partial Nuclear Test Ban Treaty. After the debacle of the Bay of Pigs, Kennedy's reputation as a tough Cold Warrior, but also a man of peace, was largely restored. Khrushchev, however, was seen by the international community and, more importantly, by the Soviet Politburo, as having retreated from a desperate situation of his own creation. He would fall from power two years later, in part because of this embarrassment. It must be noted here that part of the embarrassment stemmed from the fact that the guarantee Khrushchev received from JFK about removing Jupiter missiles from Turkey, was secret. This contributed to his perceived weakness. Cuba, though protected from future US invasion, was left feeling betrayed by the Soviets. Their relationship would never be the same again.

HISTORIOGRAPHY

"We now know… that in addition to nuclear-armed ballistic missiles, the Soviet Union had deployed 100 tactical nuclear weapons to Cuba, and the local Soviet commander there could have launched these weapons without additional codes or commands from Moscow."

Graham T. Allison
The Cuban Missile Crisis at 50

WHERE TO FIND OUT MORE

The Fog of War
Documentary by Errol Morris

Thirteen Days
Robert F. Kennedy

bit.ly/39Yi8nr

THE CUBAN MISSILE CRISIS:
the 'knot of war'

On the 14th October 1962, Major Richard Heyser – piloting a U2 spyplane 70,000 feet above western Cuba – took 928 photographs which revealed the construction of a Soviet SS-4 medium-range nuclear missile site. The next 13 days saw the world on the edge of nuclear war

www.versushistory.com   @versushistory

WHY DID KHRUSHCHEV PLACE MISSILES IN CUBA?

- TO NEGOTIATE WITH JFK
- TO REMOVE AMERICA'S 'FIRST STRIKE' CAPABILITY
- TO TRAP THE US INTO A NUCLEAR CONFLICT
- TO DEFEND CUBA
- TO TEST JFK'S RESOLVE

WHAT WERE KENNEDY'S OPTIONS?

- DO NOTHING
- A 'SURGICAL' AIR STRIKE TO REMOVE THE MISSILES
- INVADE CUBA
- USE DIPLOMATIC PRESSURES
- BLOCKADE CUBA

EXECUTIVE COMMITTEE OF THE NATIONAL SECURITY COUNCIL (ExComm)

JFK convened this committee to advise on the options open to him and to AVOID another humiliation – albeit infinitely more dangerous – like the Bay of Pigs

+ 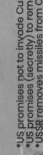 =

*US promises not to invade Cuba
*US promises (secretly) to remove Jupiter missiles from Turkey
*USSR removes missiles from Cuba

"Mr. President, we and you ought not now to pull on the ends of the rope in which you have tied the knot of war...and what that would mean is not for me to explain to you..."

Soviet Premier Khrushchev

SHOOTING FOR THE STARS

OVERVIEW

Unthinkable only a few years previously, the launch of Sputnik, Yuri Gagarin's flight and the success of Apollo 11, were seen as testament to humanity's vision and greatness. In the Cold War context these achievements were also interpreted, by extension, as a testament to the vision and greatness of the superpower responsible for them. Consequently, there was significant international prestige to be gained by 'winning' the race to dominate space. Yet the space race was also deeply military in nature. Highly dependent on military technology – Sputnik was launched by an adapted Soviet R7 missile – the military potential of developments in space technology also provided a key justification for funding. This justification was critical given NASA consumed over 4% of federal funding at its peak.

SIGNIFICANCE

The achievements of the space race were monumental. At the height of the Space Race, technology was simply not sufficiently developed for anything in orbit to be of practical military value. Moreover, the Outer Space Treaty, signed in 1967, banned the positioning of weapons in space, and American attempts to create a space-based missile shield in the 1980's ran into similar technological barriers. While developments in launch technology did overlap with military missile programs, the primary significance of the space race lay in its propaganda value. As a manifestation of a nation's technological sophistication, the Space Race was unmatched, while the way it captured the global imagination showcased its reach. In this sense, a victory in the space race was a prime demonstration of 'soft power'.

HISTORIOGRAPHY

"This competition prompted each nation to allocate vast human and economic resources for space exploration. In the end though...Ultimate success rested on the technological, industrial and organisational capacities to sustain a coherent space program."

Von Hardesty and Gene Eisman
Epic Rivalry: The Inside Story of the Soviet and American Space Race

WHERE TO FIND OUT MORE

Space Race: The Epic Battle Between America and the Soviet Union for...Space
Deborah Cadbury

Hidden Figures: The American Dream and the Untold Story of the Black Women Mathematicians Who Helped Win the Space Race
Margot Lee Shetterly

bit.ly/2DB9wHB

THE SPACE RACE

As the Cold War got under way, both the US and the USSR looked for areas in which they could assert their dominance. For two decades outer-space became the new Cold War battleground - metaphorically as well as literally.

Sputnik

On 4th October 1957, the USSR launched the world's first manmade satellite into space. Sputnik, which is the Russian word for 'traveller', was placed into earth's orbit and emitted radio pulses for three weeks before its batteries ran out. It's success alarmed the Americans and kick-started the space race.

NASA

Partly as a result of Sputnik, President Eisenhower signed the National Aeronautics and Space Act on 29th July 1958, creating the National Aeronautics and Space Administration (NASA).

Yuri Gagarin

On 12th April 1961 Soviet Cosmonaut - Yuri Gagarin - became the first person to orbit the earth. This was an astounding achievement and acted as another stimulus in the race to conquer space.

JFK

In May 1961 President Kennedy announces his plan to put a man on the moon within a decade. The Apollo programme was created by NASA within a year.

The Moon

In July 1969 America 'won' the race to the Moon when Neil Armstrong and 'Buzz' Aldrin walked on its surface.

Apollo-Soyuz

Enthusiasm began to wane until the 'handshake in space' between US and Soviet astronauts in this mission of 1975.

www.VersusHistory.com
@VersusHistory
#VersusHistory

WELCOME TO THE JUNGLE

OVERVIEW

American involvement in Vietnam is not an easy topic to provide an 'overview' for. There was no formal declaration of war by the United States on North Vietnam; involvement was gradual, complex, and multi-causal; entanglement spanned a number of presidencies; and the outcomes are disputed. If one is to pinpoint the start of US involvement anywhere, then it may as well be with the defeat of the French at Dien Bien Phu – although this choice is not without its difficulties. The Americans became concerned that French defeat against the Vietminh – who were looking to unite Vietnam under their ideology of communist national self-determination – might foreshadow the 'falling' of other Asian countries to communism. The 'domino theory', as it was described, became the 'raison d'être' for American interest – in all of its manifestations – in Vietnam. At the height of the conflict, well over half a million US soldiers had their boots on the ground. In 1973, after nearly 60,000 American deaths and Vietnamese casualties in their millions, Peace Accords were signed in Paris, and America agreed to withdraw.

SIGNIFICANCE

Unlike in Korea, American intervention in Vietnam was, by and large, unilateral. As a result, any praise or criticism would be left solely at the door of the Americans. In fact, as the conflict wore on, international condemnation – from allies and enemies alike – was loud and vociferous. Even at home, the 'television war' sowed the seeds of division among the American people, effectively destroying the broad public Cold War consensus of support for their government's policies. Although justified by many at the time and since, often using the threat of communist expansion, the need for containment in Asia, and *realpolitik*, American adventurism in Vietnam – with all of its tragic consequences – damaged the reputation of the US as a protector of freedom. American loss in a proxy war without any tangible benefits – the North ultimately overran the South and accomplished their goal – was a disaster for US Cold War policy and for the people of Vietnam.

HISTORIOGRAPHY

"A new humility and a new sophistication may form the best parts of a complex heritage left to the Army by the long, bitter war in Vietnam."

Vincent H. Demma
The US Army in Vietnam

WHERE TO FIND OUT MORE

American Involvement in the Vietnam War: Nothing to Declare
Elliott L. Watson (bit.ly/3iish1i)

Examining Issues Through Political Cartoons: The Vietnam War
Louise Gerdes

bit.ly/2XwldFk

THE VIETNAM WAR

WWW.VERSUSHISTORY.COM   @VERSUSHISTORY

1954	1963	1964	1965	1968	1968	1973	1975
DIEN BIEN PHU	DIEM ASSASSINATED	GULF OF TONKIN INCIDENT	OPERATION ROLLING THUNDER BEGINS	MY LAI MASSACRE	TET OFFENSIVE	PARIS PEACE ACCORDS	FALL OF SAIGON

$168 BILLION

The cost of the war to the USA. Equivalent to over $1 Trillion today

75 MILES

The length of one tunnel system, the Cu Chi tunnels, constructed by the Vietcong

AFRICAN-AMERICANS MADE UP

12.5% of US casualties
11% of US soldiers
2% of US officers

260 MILLION

The number of bombs dropped on neighbouring Laos in the course of the conflict, equivalent to one every 8 minutes, or 7 for each man, woman and child in the country

US PERSONNEL IN VIETNAM

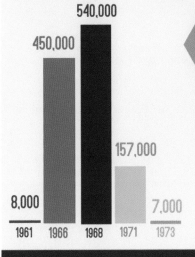

- 450,000
- 540,000
- 157,000
- 8,000
- 7,000

1961 1966 1968 1971 1973

50KM

The width of Vietnam at its narrowest point near Danang, where the US targeted the Ho Chi Minh trail

2,000,000	1,100,000	254,256	58,318
CIVILIAN CASUALTIES	NORTH VIETNAMESE AND VIETCONG FIGHTERS	SOUTH VIETNAMESE SOLDIERS	US SOLDIERS

ESTIMATES OF WAR CASUALTIES*

*Some of these figures are disputed

BLOOMING LIBERAL

OVERVIEW

As with many of the countries behind the 'Iron Curtain', Czechoslovakia was expected to adhere strictly to the Soviet-ordained political and economic model of communist centralisation. This, along with the overt Russian exploitation of Czech resources and its means of production, led to economic privation and a tightly controlled population. When Alexander Dubcek became the First Secretary of the Communist Party, he set about a reformist agenda of greater rights for his people, the promise of future democratic elections, economic consumerism, as well as greater comity with the West. Collectively, Dubcek named these reforms, 'socialism with a human face', although they became more popularly known as the 'Prague Spring' reforms. Inevitably, these reforms lasted as long as it took the USSR to mobilise three quarters of a million soldiers to invade and 'restore' control.

SIGNIFICANCE

The Prague Spring revealed, in a manner not dissimilar to Hungary in 1956, the structural weaknesses inherent in the Soviet-mandated model of centralised economics and politics within its satellite states. As in Hungary, the dire economic situation in Czechoslovakia, coupled with the ever-increasing erosion of individual liberty, led to attempts at reform. More than this, as spontaneous public resistance to the invasion rapidly spread across the country, it became clear that civilian-based resistance – exemplified by Jan Palach's tragic self-immolation – was a clear threat to Soviet influence everywhere. Indeed, even within Russia, small protests erupted at the heavy-handed response of Brezhnev. China, once one of the USSR's staunchest allies, condemned Russian actions. Having said this, the Prague Spring revealed a generational split between old-guard Czech conservative communists and their younger, more liberal brethren; not everybody despised Soviet-control in Czechoslovakia. The Soviet reaction to the Prague Spring is probably the most notable outcome of it – Brezhnev re-energised Russian control over the Warsaw Pact countries in, what became known as, the Brezhnev Doctrine. This also helped re-energise the Cold War.

HISTORIOGRAPHY

"Moscow succeeded in restoring the supremacy of the state, but the ultimate cost of victory was high."

Marc Santora
50 Years After Prague Spring, Lessons on Freedom (and a Broken Spirit)

WHERE TO FIND OUT MORE

The 1968 Czechoslovak Crisis: Reconsidering its History and Politics
Maud Bracke

The Prague Spring and its Aftermath
Kieran Williams

bit.ly/3ibXT8N

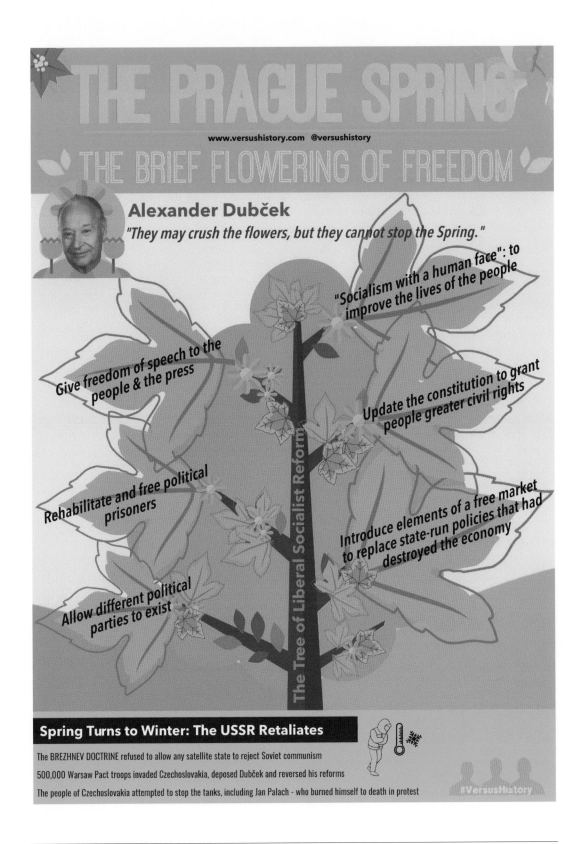

THE PRAGUE SPRING

www.versushistory.com @versushistory

THE BRIEF FLOWERING OF FREEDOM

Alexander Dubček
"They may crush the flowers, but they cannot stop the Spring."

"Socialism with a human face": to improve the lives of the people

Give freedom of speech to the people & the press

Update the constitution to grant people greater civil rights

Rehabilitate and free political prisoners

Introduce elements of a free market to replace state-run policies that had destroyed the economy

Allow different political parties to exist

The Tree of Liberal Socialist Reform

Spring Turns to Winter: The USSR Retaliates

The BREZHNEV DOCTRINE refused to allow any satellite state to reject Soviet communism

500,000 Warsaw Pact troops invaded Czechoslovakia, deposed Dubček and reversed his reforms

The people of Czechoslovakia attempted to stop the tanks, including Jan Palach - who burned himself to death in protest

#VersusHistory

INTO AFRICA

OVERVIEW

Struggles for independence, often followed by internal power struggles after imperial departures from Africa, proved a fertile breeding ground for Cold War conflict. With both superpowers keen to expand their spheres of influence, contain the other side, as well as monopolise local resources – such as Congo's Uranium – many proxy wars were fought across the African continent. In each of the conflicts indicated in the infographic opposite, most of which lasted decades, support was given to the opposing sides by communist states (though not always the USSR) and Western powers. In some cases, proxy wars were lent support by west-aligned, white minority regimes, such as those in South Africa and Rhodesia.

SIGNIFICANCE

Proxy wars in parts of Africa created significant devastation for populations. Casualty numbers from the conflicts themselves were always high. However, the drawn out and brutal nature of many of the civil conflicts also exacerbated social, agricultural, or environmental problems, leading to extended and widespread suffering for the local populations. Yet, for all the destruction they caused, Africa was only ever a minor consideration for the two superpowers; neither would get 'boots on the ground' and the USA's strategy of containment was only loosely applied. Tellingly, it was Fidel Castro, rather than the leaders of either superpower, who was most often held in esteem by African leaders.

HISTORIOGRAPHY

"The increasingly important international role of the Soviet Union made many radical African leaders see Moscow as the global socialist counterweight to the United States"

The Global Cold War
Odd Arne Westad

WHERE TO FIND OUT MORE

Foreign intervention in Africa: From the Cold War to the War on Terror
Elizabeth Schmidt

Good Guys, Bad Guys ep. 17 The Cold War
CNN documentary series

bit.ly/3iblXbX

The Cold War in Africa – the hotspots

External influencers:

Cuba

Cuba sent significant forces to bolster fellow 'liberation movements', with 40,000 troops stationed in Angola and 15,000 sent to Ethiopia

The UN

UN forces played key roles in the Congo Crisis. Initially acting as peacekeepers, they took a more direct, interventionist role from 1961

United Nations

Portugal

A number of the conflicts that occurred did so in former Portuguese territories. Angola and Mozambique formed Marxist governments after independence in 1975

1960-64
Congo

Civil war broke out after independence from Belgium in 1960. The conflict involved the UN, and saw army Colonel Joseph Mobuto lead Congo with western backing until 1991

1974-91
Ethiopia

Emperor Haile Selassie was removed in a coup of 1974, led by the Derg, a Soviet-backed Marxist military dictatorship. Soviet and Cuban aid was used in the Ogaden War with neighbouring Somalia and in an on-off civil war which lasted until 1991

1977-92
Mozambique

After independence, the communist FRELIMO party formed a government, but fought a 15 year, 1 million casualty, civil war with the anti-communist RENAMO rebels. RENAMO were supported by neighbouring Rhodesia (Zimbabwe) and the apartheid regime in South Africa

1975-92
Angola

After the Portuguese departure, two former anti Portuguese groups fought for control, the communist MPLA and anti communist UNITA. Conflict dragged on until a power-sharing agreement in 1992

BACKYARD BULLIES

OVERVIEW

The USA's Monroe Doctrine warned that the Americas should exist in a "free and independent condition". Such a situation, with the USA as guarantor, reflected the sense that the USA considered Latin America its own backyard; within its own sphere of influence. Yet a certain irony would develop during the Cold War with many accusing the USA of being the key obstacle to such a condition of freedom from outside intervention. With the growth of left-wing groups and the real danger of revolution in a number of states, the USA saw threats to both their commercial and strategic hegemony in Latin America. To preserve this hegemony, the USA brokered the Rio Defence Treaty in 1947. However, US intervention, whether open or covert, economic or military, at the invitation of, or in opposition to, the wishes of Latin American governments, was a recurring feature, across the entirety of the Cold War.

SIGNIFICANCE

For the majority of the Cold War, Latin America was, in the eyes of the superpowers at least, a secondary sphere. This was reflected by comparatively low levels of expenditure, and in part due to its existing condition as an American sphere of influence. However, for many, US actions in the region were significant to the wider Cold War in undermining the narrative of 'good' America against the 'evil, expansionist, imperialist' USSR. The USA's involvement in numerous coups, subversion of democracy in defence of 'friendly' dictators, and the supplying of paramilitaries, meant that the citizens of Berlin and Bogota faced starkly different experiences of the USA.

HISTORIOGRAPHY

"Internal and external turmoil became near-permanent features of Latin American affairs. Superpower rivalry, foreign intervention and inter-American diplomatic strife dominated Latin America's external relations."

Hal Brands
Latin America's Cold War

WHERE TO FIND OUT MORE

Beyond the Eagle's Shadow: New Histories of Latin America's Cold War
Virginia Garrard-Burnett, Mark Atwood Lawrence & Julio E. Moreno (eds.)

Latin America and the Global Cold War
Thomas C. Field, Stella Krepp & Vanni Pettina (eds.)

bit.ly/30u3Ily

THE COLD WAR IN LATIN AMERICA

% of US foreign aid being given to Latin American nations

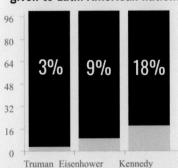

Truman	3%
Eisenhower	9%
Kennedy	18%

(Y-axis: 0, 16, 32, 48, 64, 80, 96)

1823

The Monroe Doctrine of 1823, originally framed in opposition to European colonialism in the Americas, had a big influence on the Cold War. It was cited as a justification for opposing Soviet influence and providing military and financial aid to anti-communist governments in Latin America

Countries where there was direct US involvement

CUBA | DOMINICAN REPUBLIC | GUYANA (FORMERLY BRITISH GUIANA) | CHILE | NICARAGUA | EL SALVADOR | PANAMA | GUATEMALA | BRAZIL

Kennedy's Alliance for Progress

10 years
10 year plan to encourage development using US Aid

$22.3 bn
$22.3 billion was the estimated total amount sent to Latin America by the early 1970s

6 coups
6 coups in 1963 alone and by the 1970's 13 governments had been replaced by military rule

"Political freedom must accompany material progress. Our Alliance for Progress is an alliance of free governments and it must work to eliminate tyranny from a hemisphere in which it has no place."

JFK, March 13th 1961

President Carter and Panama

78%
The percentage of the public who opposed transferring control of the Panama Canal to Panama

31.12.1999
The date agreed by Carter & Torrijos for handover of the Canal to Panama. This was signed in 1977

President Nixon and Chile

$10 million
Amount of money granted to the CIA for use in trying to stop Allende winning the 1970 election. It failed

300%
Inflation under Allende. Nixon said he wanted 'to make the economy scream' by withdrawing aid

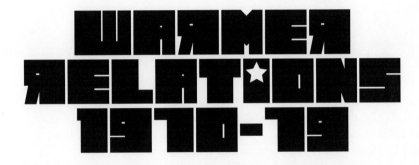

BREAKING THE ICE

OVERVIEW

After almost twenty-five years of Cold War confrontation, the two superpowers briefly evolved a less tense relationship during the 1970's. Using the French word 'détente', meaning 'relaxation', to describe this evolution, both the United States and the Soviet Union took active steps to improve their Cold War diplomacy with one another. Between 1969 and 1975, Leonid Brezhnev, Richard Nixon, and Henry Kissinger orchestrated a series of developments – from summits to nuclear non-proliferation agreements – designed to reduce the demands placed on each country by the Cold War, as well as the threat posed by a nuclear exchange.

SIGNIFICANCE

Although it was short-lived, the détente of the 1970's was unprecedented in its scope and aims. Although much of the fanfare surrounding the more convivial relationship focused on the humanitarian drive to reduce the potential for nuclear war, there were far more complex motivations at play. And it is perhaps from here where this iteration of détente derives its significance. As was the case with the Marshall and Molotov Plans, the surface humanitarianism of détente was underpinned by strategic imperatives. Both the US and the USSR had serious social and economic issues that were being exacerbated by the cost – in both money and energies – of the Cold War. With the Vietnam War and the Sino-Soviet split as a backdrop, both sides were looking for a way to alleviate the burdens of the Cold War. In a very real sense, détente in the 1970's was driven by a tacit acknowledgement by both sides that a 'timeout' was required. For a brief period in the Cold War, there was a broad consensus of hope that a corner had been turned. Little could anyone have known at the time, but around this 'corner' was fifteen years of much worse.

HISTORIOGRAPHY

"Détente did not happen in a vacuum."

Brian K. Muzas
Jimmy Carter, Ronald Reagan, and the End (or Consummation) of Détente

WHERE TO FIND OUT MORE

The Concept of Détente
Brian White

The World in a Word: The Rise and Fall of Détente
H. W. Brands

bit.ly/2PrPdid

Détente in the 1970's

Photo by Toa Heftiba on Unsplash

WHY?

The US was desperately looking for a way out of their war in Vietnam. Détente would allow America to focus on a solution.

The USSR was suffering from a desperately poor standard of living. Détente might alleviate its economic problems.

The price of oil skyrocketed, causing even further strains on the economies of the two superpowers.

The US needed to address broiling social tensions that had led to riots and protests. Détente would provide 'breathing space' to concentrate on domestic issues.

The Sino-Soviet split worried the USSR that China would begin seeking friendship with the USA. This would cause a major threat.

Both countries found the nuclear arms race to be a strain on their economies. Détente would reduce the need to continue spending on their nuclear arsenals.

www.versushistory.com @versushistory

JUST WARMING UP

OVERVIEW

From 1968-75, the USSR and the USA put pen to paper on a series of high-profile agreements that promised, among other things, the reduction of their nuclear arsenals and delivery systems, as well as the non-nuclearisation of space. Meaningful gestures were also made that sought to bring the two erstwhile opponents closer together: Nixon became the first US president to visit Moscow in 1972, while the space programs of the two superpowers combined in space for the Apollo-Soyuz mission in 1975.

SIGNIFICANCE

One question historians commonly ask themselves is the following: How much did détente actually achieve? As one can imagine, that question is as difficult as answering why détente emerged in the first place. Détente was not a monolithic entity with rigid form and substance. There was no blueprint that was followed, nor a long-term plan devised. If anything, the warmer relationship between the two superpowers could best be described as a series of ad hoc agreements that were influenced by contemporary concerns and helped fulfil immediate strategic and humanitarian goals. From nuclear non-proliferation to the 'handshake in space', détente was as much a product of its historical context as it was a product of the individuals who helped negotiate its, quite disparate, elements. However, from photo opportunities to developments of real substance, détente in this period marked an historic deviation – in many respects – from the standard model of behaviour that had heretofore characterised the Cold War. Nevertheless, even during the period of the Cold War that saw détente emerge, there was little 'slowing down' by either side trying to get the upper hand over the other. From unrelenting espionage to the 'massaging' of missile figures, the Cold War very much continued as normal – it just did so behind the scenes. Consequently, when it came to an end there was almost a sense of inevitability about its failure.

HISTORIOGRAPHY

"So long as the Soviet Union aspires to the status of a world power and regards its attained position worth holding on to…there are clear limits to the reduction of its military and armament potential."

Dieter Senghaas
U.S.-Soviet Rivalry and the Problem of Peace

WHERE TO FIND OUT MORE

What course for the Kremlin in the 1970's?
'Great Decisions Journal' No.115

Soviet Perceptions of U.S. "Positions-of-Strength" Diplomacy in the 1970s
William B. Husband

bit.ly/39Xt70x

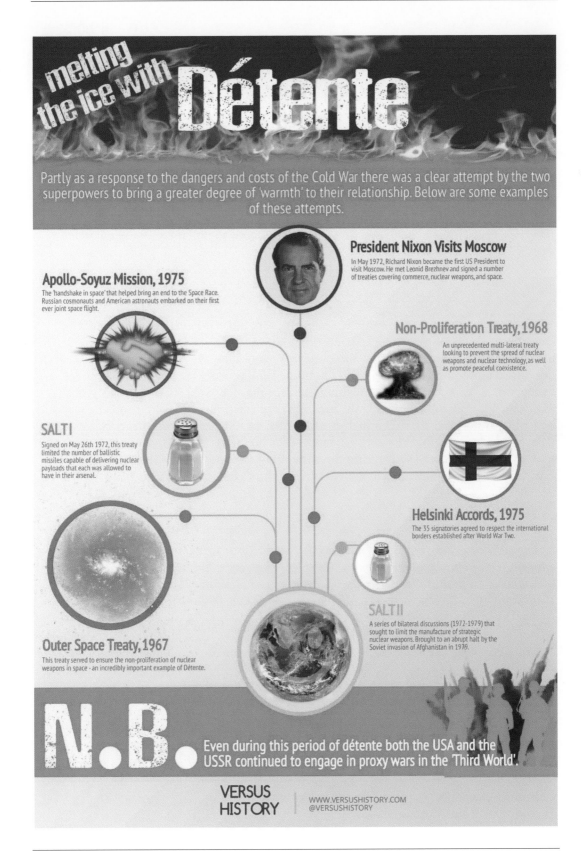

melting the ice with Détente

Partly as a response to the dangers and costs of the Cold War there was a clear attempt by the two superpowers to bring a greater degree of 'warmth' to their relationship. Below are some examples of these attempts.

President Nixon Visits Moscow
In May 1972, Richard Nixon became the first US President to visit Moscow. He met Leonid Brezhnev and signed a number of treaties covering commerce, nuclear weapons, and space.

Apollo-Soyuz Mission, 1975
The 'handshake in space' that helped bring an end to the Space Race. Russian cosmonauts and American astronauts embarked on their first ever joint space flight.

Non-Proliferation Treaty, 1968
An unprecedented multi-lateral treaty looking to prevent the spread of nuclear weapons and nuclear technology, as well as promote peaceful coexistence.

SALT I
Signed on May 26th 1972, this treaty limited the number of ballistic missiles capable of delivering nuclear payloads that each was allowed to have in their arsenal.

Helsinki Accords, 1975
The 35 signatories agreed to respect the international borders established after World War Two.

SALT II
A series of bilateral discussions (1972-1979) that sought to limit the manufacture of strategic nuclear weapons. Brought to an abrupt halt by the Soviet invasion of Afghanistan in 1979.

Outer Space Treaty, 1967
This treaty served to ensure the non-proliferation of nuclear weapons in space - an incredibly important example of Détente.

N.B.
Even during this period of détente both the USA and the USSR continued to engage in proxy wars in the 'Third World'.

VERSUS HISTORY

WWW.VERSUSHISTORY.COM
@VERSUSHISTORY

EASTERN PROMISES

OVERVIEW

The brainchild of Willy Brandt, who served as Foreign Minister of West Germany from 1966 and Chancellor from 1969, Ostpolitik saw a recalibration of West Germany's relations with the East. This new philosophy placed rapprochement and normalisation as foreign policy priorities and led to a series of treaties signed with the USSR and satellite states. The treaties renounced the use of force, established formal diplomatic relations for the first time and confirmed the existing territorial status quo, ending disputes with Poland. Critically, the countries with whom relations were normalised included East Germany, with whom the Basic Treaty was signed in 1972, paving the way for both to join the UN the following year.

SIGNIFICANCE

While some, particularly domestically, criticised Ostpolitik for its conciliatory tone, Brandt saw it as a long-term strategy to undermine communism. Arguably, Brandt's Ostpolitik came out of the deep-seated desire for long term reunification that neither partition in 1945, nor formal separation for 20 years, had diminished among the average German. For many of its supporters 'Wandel durch Annäherung' (change through rapprochement) saw engagement as key to highlighting the inherent contradictions in socialism and encourage a desire for change in the East. His policy was lauded on the international stage and saw Brandt awarded the Nobel Peace Prize in 1971 for his efforts. In the longer term, the large-scale protests of the late 1980s against the communist system in the GDR and Eastern Europe, could be considered a fulfilment of Ostpolitik's long term strategy.

HISTORIOGRAPHY

"After 1969 the rules of the game changed...Brandt's Ostpolitik represented a... fundamental alteration of German foreign policy... The FRG had ceased to be a revisionist power politically... the end was no longer to undo the results of World War Two but to accept them and induce improvements in intra-German relations within the status quo."

Angela Stent
From Embargo to Ostpolitik: The Political Economy of West German - Soviet Relations 1955-1980

WHERE TO FIND OUT MORE

Reconciliation Road: Willy Brandt, Ostpolitik and the Quest for European Peace
Benedikt Schoenborn

Germany Since 1945: Politics, Culture and Society
Peter Caldwell and Karrin Hanshew

bit.ly/3gvHAL

OSTPOLITIK

West Germany's 'New Eastern Policy'

FEATURES OF WEST GERMANY'S

Relations between East and West Germany should be on the...

"...basis of equality, guaranteeing their mutual territorial integrity as well as the border between them, and recognizing each other's independence and sovereignty".

BASIC TREATY, SIGNED 1972

BILATERAL TREATIES

4 SIGNED WITH NEIGHBOURS

USSR
CZECHOSLOVAKIA
GDR
POLAND

RECOGNISING LEGAL STATUS OF EAST GERMANY

MAINTAINING COMMITMENT TO NATO

ABANDONING PRE 1945 TERRITORIAL CLAIMS

EXPANDING TRADE LINKS WITH USSR

The Rise of Willy Brandt

1966 Appointed W. Germany's Foreign Minister

1969 Elected Chancellor of W. Germany

1970 Awarded the Nobel Peace Prize

www.versushistory.com @versushistory

ATOMIC SEASON(ING)

OVERVIEW

The SALT I Treaty, signed in Moscow in May 1972, was the culmination of three years of talks between the USA and USSR. Arising from the new spirit of détente, it was the first treaty to attempt to limit the nuclear arsenal of the two superpowers. In an attempt to slow down and limit the crippling cost of the Arms Race, Brezhnev and Nixon signed an agreement freezing various elements of their nuclear capabilities, including Inter Continental Ballistic Missiles, Submarine Launched Ballistic Missiles and Anti-Ballistic Missiles, for the next five years,

SIGNIFICANCE

SALT I's significance rests more in its symbolic value than the practical merits of the limitations it imposed. That SALT I failed to restrict the development of new weapons systems meant it did not halt spending or the arms race, and the allowed weapons of both sides were enough to unleash destruction on an apocalyptic level. However, as the first arms limitation agreement signed in the Cold War, it was evidence that the new zeitgeist could lead to concrete progress, and that détente was about more than rhetoric. It helped pave the way for a series of agreements in the 1970's which included, but also moved beyond, further restrictions on arms.

HISTORIOGRAPHY

"The SALT I agreement that was finally signed in 1972 froze ICBM deployment but not MIRV, which was about as meaningful as freezing the cavalry of European countries in 1938, but not the tanks. Throughout the period of the Nixon administration, the Pentagon added three warheads each day to the MIRV arsenal...by 1977 the United States had ten thousand warheads, the Russians four thousand. It was a strange way to control the arms race."

★MIRV's could carry 3-10 nuclear warheads on a single missile.

Stephen Ambrose
Rise to Globalism: American Foreign Policy Since 1938, 9th ed.

WHERE TO FIND OUT MORE

The Rise and Fall of Détente: American Foreign Policy and the Transformation…Cold War
Jussi Hanhimaki

A Tangled Web: The Making of Foreign Policy in the Nixon Presidency
William Bundy

bit.ly/2XvAQxK

WHAT YOU NEED TO KNOW

ABOUT

SALT I, 1972

WHAT'S IN A NAME?

S **A** **L** **T**

STRATEGIC | ARMS | LIMITATION | TALKS

AGREEMENTS

ONLY 2 ANTI BALLISTIC MISSILE SITES EACH

USE OF SATELLITES TO MONITOR ADHERENCE

5 YEAR FREEZE ON ICBMS:
USSR - 1618
USA - 1054

5 YEAR FREEZE ON SLBMS:
USSR - 740
USA - 740

BASIC PRINCIPLES FOR CONDUCTING NUCLEAR WARFARE

LIMITATIONS

1. NO RESTRICTIONS ON NEWER TECHNOLOGIES

2. BASIC PRINCIPLES AGREEMENT DEPENDENT ON IDEALISM

3. STRATEGIC BOMBERS NOT INCLUDED

4. A FREEZE FAILED TO NEGATE THE FACT BOTH SIDES HAD ENORMOUS STOCKPILES ALREADY

5. AMERICAN CRITICS COMPLAINED IT ENTRENCHED A SOVIET NUMERICAL ADVANTAGE

"(SALT I is) the beginning of a process that is enormously important that will limit now, and, we hope, later reduce the burden of arms, and thereby reduce the danger of war"

Richard Nixon, US President, 1972

HOW SALT I FITS INTO THE WIDER PICTURE OF THE ARMS RACE

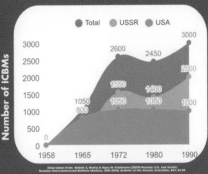

Data taken from Robert S. Norris & Hans M. Kristensen (2009) Nuclear U.S. and Soviet/ Russian Intercontinental Ballistic Missiles, 1959-2008, Bulletin of the Atomic Scientists, 65:1, 62-69

WWW.VERSUSHISTORY.COM | @VERSUSHISTORY

HELSINKI: A BASKET CASE

OVERVIEW

Building on the achievements of earlier agreements, the Helsinki 'Conference on Security and Cooperation in Europe' was the most wide-ranging agreement of détente. The Accords signed after three years of almost solid discussion covered the diverse areas of human rights, scientific and technological cooperation, and European security. In the wake of the Brezhnev Doctrine of 1968, the Soviet Union remained keen to consolidate power in its sphere of influence. The variety in Helsinki's 'baskets' allowed the USSR to make concessions in human rights, while achieving Brezhnev's overriding priority by formalising the borders of Europe and cementing the Kremlin's hold over the satellite states.

SIGNIFICANCE

None of the Helsinki accords stood the test of time. Within a few years there were complaints from the US about Soviet violations of the agreements on human rights. That the USSR could implement these agreements as and when it desired, meant that little had changed. In addition, the formation of 'Helsinki groups' to monitor Soviet adherence, only created further tension. Although cooperation was seen in such things as the Apollo-Soyuz mission, which showed visible symbols of progress, these positive developments would decline, along with détente itself, following the Soviet invasion of Afghanistan. While the agreements on borders would last until the end of the Cold War, later events would show the Kremlin's, and therefore Helsinki's, focus was wrong; internal dissatisfaction, rather than western interference, would be the greater threat to the Soviet sphere of influence.

HISTORIOGRAPHY

"The signing of the Final Act of the Conference… in Helsinki in 1975 was a paradoxical event in the history of the Cold War. At the time widely considered a Soviet triumph, many historians now believe that the Final Act was a milestone in the eventual collapse of Communism in Europe."

Robert Brier
"Beyond the Helsinki Effect"

WHERE TO FIND OUT MORE

The Final Act: The Helsinki Accords and the Transformation of the Cold War
Michael Cotey Morgan

The Helsinki Effect: International Norms, Human Rights, and the Demise of Communism
Daniel C. Thomas

bit.ly/3keiiMm

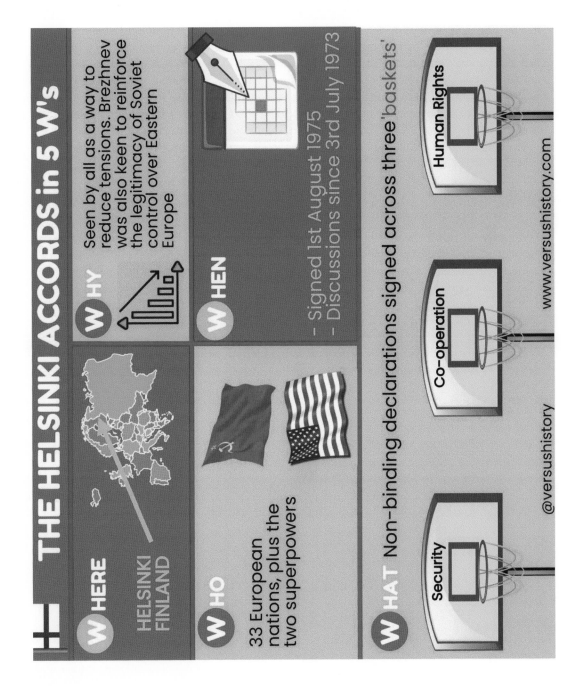

THE HELSINKI ACCORDS in 5 W's

WHERE
HELSINKI
FINLAND

WHO
33 European nations, plus the two superpowers

WHY
Seen by all as a way to reduce tensions. Brezhnev was also keen to reinforce the legitimacy of Soviet control over Eastern Europe

WHEN
- Signed 1st August 1975
- Discussions since 3rd July 1973

WHAT Non-binding declarations signed across three 'baskets'

Security

Co-operation

Human Rights

@versushistory

www.versushistory.com

TABLE MANNERS

OVERVIEW

After a coincidental boarding of the Chinese table tennis team bus by USA player Glenn Cowan at the World Championships in Japan, the US team were invited to visit China in April 1971. Political visits by Secretary of State Henry Kissinger in July and October, and President Nixon in February 1972, followed and a series of agreements struck. As a result, the 1970's saw Sino-US relations transformed. This was largely due to a new alignment of interests following the Sino-Soviet split of the late 1960's, but rapprochement also served domestic interests; in the US Nixon wanted a diplomatic success to distract from the quagmire in Vietnam, while for the PRC it was a chance to enhance prestige and lift a US imposed trade embargo.

SIGNIFICANCE

Significantly for today's world, the diplomatic reset of the 1970's saw China begin its ascent to prominence on the world stage, as she benefitted more tangibly from rapprochement than the US. With America not exercising its veto power, the People's Republic of China replaced Taiwan on the UN Security Council. In what was a significant reversal of previous US policy, Washington's recognition the 'One China' policy enhanced Chinese claims to Taiwan. Rapprochement also affected the wider Cold War. Fears of a potential US-China alliance may have been a factor in encouraging Brezhnev and the USSR to sign SALT I in 1972, while North Vietnamese diplomats felt an added motivation to end the war with the USA were China to decrease their aid.

HISTORIOGRAPHY

"China brought twenty years of confrontation and mutual suspicion to an end; promoted normalization of bilateral relations...increased China's diplomatic political manoeuvring room; and advanced its international position."

Gong Li
Re-examining the Cold War: US-China Diplomacy, 1954-73 (eds. R. Ross & C. Jiang)

WHERE TO FIND OUT MORE

Ping Pong Diplomacy: The Secret History Behind the Game That Changed the World
Nicholas Griffin

Negotiating with the Enemy: U.S.-China Talks during the Cold War 1949-1972
Yafeng Xia

bit.ly/31qosQK

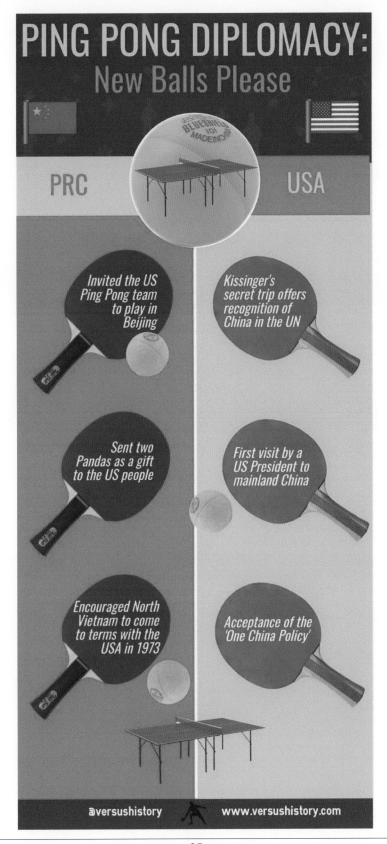

THE SECOND COLD WAR 1979-89

COLD WAR: THE SEQUEL

OVERVIEW

It is no exaggeration to say that the 1970's brought a real optimism that the Cold War rivalry which had so dominated the global landscape since 1945, might actually subside. Détente became a reality – albeit a conditional one – as both the USSR and the USA began laying productive foundations for, what might end up being, a peaceful coexistence. Having said this, détente in the 1970's was a fragile entity, and one which could always collapse. And collapse it did, because of a complex mix of factors, including the Soviet invasion of Afghanistan, the election of Ronald Reagan as US president, and the Islamic Revolution in Iran. What replaced détente was a period of Cold War tension to rival any that had come before it, and what many historians termed, the 'Second Cold War'.

SIGNIFICANCE

One thing the 'Second Cold War' revealed was that the détente of the 1970's was not as successful as it may have been heralded at the time. It became clear that, while SALT I and II represented progress on the issue of nuclear non-proliferation, and public summits between the superpowers appeared genuine, beneath the surface of that veneer, mistrust and covert operations designed to destabilise the sphere of influence of one another, continued unabated. Ronald Reagan made it a tenet of his 'doctrine' that containment of communism – a mainstay of US foreign policy since 1945 – should be expanded to the 'rolling back' of communism. Reagan's vocal hatred for the USSR – epitomised in his 'Evil Empire' speech – reignited the Cold War, and his massive increase in military spending (nearly half a trillion dollars in 1985) dared the Soviet Union to keep up. Ultimately, the 'Second Cold War', driven as it was by an arms race the Soviet Union could not afford, helped catalyse the collapse of the USSR and the end of the Cold War, but not before the fear of nuclear annihilation had once again spread across the world.

HISTORIOGRAPHY

"(Reagan was) …the first postwar President to take the offensive both ideologically and strategically."

Henry Kissinger
Diplomacy

WHERE TO FIND OUT MORE

Three Days in Moscow: Ronald Reagan and the Fall of the Soviet Empire
Brett Baier and Catherine Whitney

The Cold War: A New History
John Lewis Gaddis

bit.ly/3khDy3C

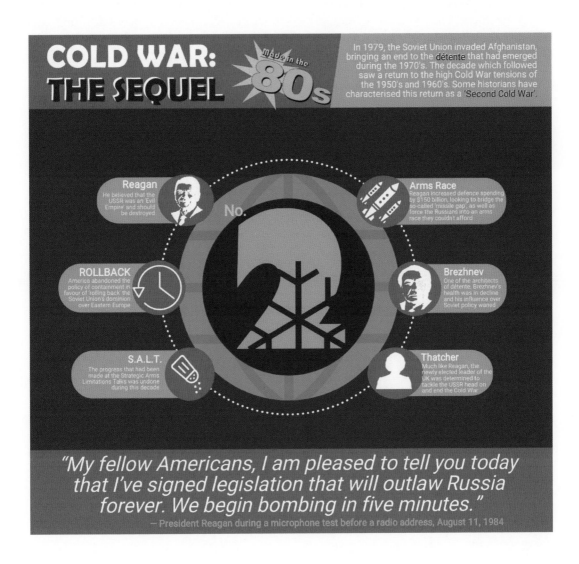

COLD WAR:
THE SEQUEL
Made in the
80s
In 1979, the Soviet Union invaded Afghanistan, bringing an end to the détente that had emerged during the 1970's. The decade which followed saw a return to the high Cold War tensions of the 1950's and 1960's. Some historians have characterised this return as a 'Second Cold War'.
Reagan
He believed that the USSR was an 'Evil Empire' and should be destroyed
Arms Race
Reagan increased defence spending by $150 billion, looking to bridge the so-called 'missile gap', as well as force the Russians into an arms race they couldn't afford
No.
ROLLBACK
America abandoned the policy of containment in favour of 'rolling back' the Soviet Union's dominion over Eastern Europe
Brezhnev
One of the architects of détente, Brezhnev's health was in decline and his influence over Soviet policy waned
S.A.L.T.
The progress that had been made at the Strategic Arms Limitations Talks was undone during this decade
Thatcher
Much like Reagan, the newly elected leader of the UK was determined to tackle the USSR head on and end the Cold War
"My fellow Americans, I am pleased to tell you today that I've signed legislation that will outlaw Russia forever. We begin bombing in five minutes."
– President Reagan during a microphone test before a radio address, August 11, 1984

AN INVITATION TO INTERVENTION?

OVERVIEW

In a letter to US President Jimmy Carter, sent four days after the Soviet invasion, Leonid Brezhnev stated that the Soviet presence was due to a "request of the government of Afghanistan". It is certainly true that the situation in Afghanistan was a threatening one for the government. Following the communist takeover in 1978 there was increasing unrest and violence, largely due to the government's anti-Islamic policies. However, the idea that Soviet 'help' was a needed solution to this is questionable.

SIGNIFICANCE

To many contemporary observers and historians, the "request" was merely a pretext. Taraki, the leader who signed the 1978 'friendship treaty' with the USSR, had been assassinated and his replacement, Amin, had made no such request. Instead, greater significance is to be found in the wider geo-political issues of the time. The southern states of the USSR contained c.30 million Muslims. With the Iranian Revolution installing a theocracy earlier in 1979, and the escalating situation in Afghanistan, there were fears that Islamic fundamentalism could spread into the USSR itself. Additionally, in the Cold War context, Amin was seen as an unreliable ally; he had also approached the US for support against the Mujahideen. Any chance of Afghanistan moving out of the Soviet sphere, whether by a shift in Cold War allegiance or an Islamic revolution, was something the USSR felt it had to pre-emptively halt.

HISTORIOGRAPHY

"It may be, as some Americans have since maintained, that the Americans had no designs on Afghanistan of the kind the Russians attributed to them. But the Russians could not be sure of that at the time. So it was probably inevitable that they should now plan for the worst case."

Rodric Braithwaite
Afgantsy: The Russians in Afghanistan

WHERE TO FIND OUT MORE

The Great Gamble: The Soviet War in Afghanistan
Gregory Feifer

The Afghanistan Wars
William Maley

bit.ly/30tsjx9

Brewing up a storm in Afghanistan

1 Saur Revolution of 1978

Sees the PDPA (a Marxist, Socialist Party) overthrow the President of Afghanistan, Mohammed Daoud Khan in a coup

2 Appointment of Nur Muhammad Taraki as President

He oversees the implementation of a series of reforms outlawing many traditional islamic practices and imprisoning prominent figures

3 Friendship Treaty signed with USSR

In December 1978. This would later be used as the pretext for Soviet intervention

4 Growing unrest and uprisings

Opposition to the government's reforms takes the form of violent resistance by groups of 'Mujahideen', supporters of conservative Islamism

5 Hafizullah Amin takes over Presidency

Concluding an internal power struggle, Taraki is assassinated and the Prime Minister, Amin, takes his position

6 Attempts to revise policies

Amin undertakes attempts to moderate anti-islamic policies and reaches out to Pakistan & the USA for support

7 Soviet fears

With doubts over Amin's reliability, fears of US influence and concern of a potential spread of Islamism into the southern states of the USSR, Moscow decides to intervene

8 USSR invades on Christmas Day

Sending in 50,000 troops to 'protect' the PDPA, overthrowing Amin and replacing him with Babrak Karmal

www.versushistory.com   @versushistory

AFGHANISTAN: A DECADE OF DESTRUCTION

OVERVIEW

As many children around the world settled into an evening of expectation, excitedly awaiting what the next day – Christmas Day – might bring, the Soviet Union was deploying thousands of soldiers into Afghanistan. The year was 1979 and the date was December 24th. The aim of Brezhnev – the leader of the USSR – was to install and prop up a deeply unpopular Marxist party led by Babrak Karmal. This would, it was hoped, secure the Soviet-Afghan border against 'Muslim extremism' that had the potential to destabilise the rest of the USSR-held Muslim regions. It would also provide a potential route to the Middle East and the oil held therein. The war lasted ten years and did near incalculable damage to Afghanistan, the Soviet Union, and the prospect for a less volatile Cold War.

SIGNIFICANCE

The Soviet invasion of Afghanistan and the ten-year conflict that followed had a profound impact on the trajectory of the Cold War, the stability of the USSR, as well as the Afghan people. Perhaps the most immediate global consequence of the invasion was the death of détente and the termination of SALT II. President Carter's determination to support the people of Afghanistan against the Soviet military machine, as well as his proclamation that the protection of the American sphere of influence in the Middle East was of paramount importance, became known as the 'Carter Doctrine'. US military and financial support for the mujahideen fighting against the USSR turned the theatre of Afghanistan into another superpower proxy war. President Reagan continued and escalated American support as part of what became known as the 'Second Cold War'. The USSR spent billions of Rubles – which its faltering economy could not afford – on a war that they would go on to lose, ultimately helping in the demise of the Union. The impact of the war on Afghanistan – civilian, infrastructural, economic, political, and beyond – is almost unfathomable.

HISTORIOGRAPHY

"… the inability of the Soviet military to win the war decisively condemned it to suffer a slow bloodletting, in a process that exposed the very weaknesses of the military as well as the Soviet political structure and society.

General (Ret) Mohammad Yahya Nawroz & Lester W. Grau
The Soviet War in Afghanistan: History and Harbinger of Future War?

WHERE TO FIND OUT MORE

British and American Responses to the Soviet Invasion of Afghanistan
Gabriella Grasselli

Afgantsy
Rodric Braithwaite

bit.ly/2Ps0PSk

REFREEZING the COLD WAR

THE SOVIET INVASION OF AFGHANISTAN 1979-1989

No. of Deaths During the Soviet-Afghan War

- Soviet Soldiers
- Mujahideen
- Civilians

1000000
500000
0

15000
90000
1000000

8 Consequences of the Invasion

1. It restarted the Cold War
The Cold War, which had slowed down in the 1970's, immediately intensified.

2. It ended détente
Any progress made in the SALT talks ended. The US and the Soviets boycotted each other's Olympics.

3. Over a million people died
The loss of life, mainly of Afghan civilians, was tragic and staggering.

4. Over 5 million refugees fled
In the 1980's HALF of the world's refugees were Afghan.

5. Ronald Reagan
The American people elected a man they thought would be tougher on the USSR.

6. A second Cold War
Reagan began a massive military build-up and intensified US opposition to the USSR.

7. US assistance
The US provided billions of dollars (both secretly and publically) to Afghan opposition groups such as the Mujahideen.

8. Billions spent by the Soviets
The USSR spent c. $2 billion per year on the war. The cost helped cripple the Soviet economy.

www.versushistory.com @versushistory

#versushistory

WILD WEST

OVERVIEW

Ronald Reagan was an unconventional President. Coming from a career in the movie industry and with an evangelical background, Reagan saw the Cold War in starker terms than his immediate predecessors. To Reagan, the struggle for dominance was one of good against the 'Evil Empire' of the Soviet Union. During his administration, there occurred significant changes in the Cold War. While détente had crumbled in the last years of Carter, Reagan's actions, including a trillion-dollar defence program, meant this developed into a 'Second Cold War'. Later, as the Cold War climate shifted with the arrival of Gorbachev, Reagan's final years in office also saw the beginning of the end of the arms race.

SIGNIFICANCE

Reagan is often relegated to the role of best supporting actor in the story of the 1980s Cold War. Given the sea change that Gorbachev brought about, this is perhaps understandable. However, Reagan's policy of confrontation was critical in making Gorbachev's actions necessary. By ramping up arms spending, anti-Soviet rhetoric, and support for anti-communists globally, Reagan's actions ensured that there was no prospect of the Soviet Union merely limping on in the Cold War. Instead, the USSR's economy was so clearly incapable of maintaining the pace, that reforms were necessary if there was to be any chance of her survival as a superpower. Gorbachev or no Gorbachev, Reagan ensured there would be a final reckoning.

HISTORIOGRAPHY

"Stability in Soviet-American relations had come to be prized above all else...that made sense if one thought in static terms...Reagan, however, thought in evolutionary terms. He saw that the Soviet Union had lost its ideological appeal, that it was losing whatever economic strength it had once had, and that its survival as a superpower could no longer be taken for granted. That made stability, in his view, an outdated, even immoral, priority."

John Lewis Gaddis
Cold War

WHERE TO FIND OUT MORE

The Rebellion of Ronald Reagan: A History of the End of the Cold War
James Mann

Reagan: An American Journey
Bob Spitz

bit.ly/3ic5QuQ

ALL ABOUT
REAGAN

Ronald Reagan entered the White House in January 1981, having defeated the incumbent president - Jimmy Carter - in a landslide election. The Cold War would both intensify AND end under President Reagan

Reagan was Governor of California from 1967 to 1975

REPUBLICAN

DEVOTED CHRISTIAN EVANGELICAL

FORMER 'B' MOVIE STAR

THE 'EVIL EMPIRE'

In a speech on March 8 1983, Reagan famously called the USSR an 'evil empire'. To some this was dangerous; to others it was accurate

NUMBER OF ELECTORAL COLLEGE VOTES WON BY REAGAN COMPARED TO CARTER IN THE 1980 ELECTION

49

489

70%

Reagan's public approval rating on the last day of his presidency

27.3%

...of all public expenditure was spent on defence by 1988

THE REAGAN DOCTRINE

He began actively supporting anti-communist regimes around the world. Many of these were brutal dictatorships. However, these actions are often counted as key causes of the collapse of the USSR

A 'SECOND COLD WAR'

Reagan has often been accused of restarting the Cold War after the détente of the 1970's, by escalating the arms race and the space race, while simultaneously using inflammatory rhetoric

Photo Library of Congress

THE PHANTOM MENACE

OVERVIEW

The Strategic Defence Initiative, dubbed 'Star Wars' by US media, sought to give the USA security from Soviet nuclear capabilities. Announced by Reagan in 1983 as a plan to develop the ability to 'intercept and destroy strategic ballistic missiles before they reached our own soil or that of our allies', SDI encompassed various proposals for achieving this. Both ground-based and space-based systems – utilising missiles and lasers – were considered and investment was significant. SDI research and development continued beyond the end of the Cold War, until being halted by the Clinton administration in 1993.

SIGNIFICANCE

Judged against Reagan's stated aims, SDI was a failure. While tests were conducted, including successfully intercepting missiles beyond the earth's atmosphere, no comprehensive system ever materialised; indeed, some involved in the project suggested technology was decades away from such capabilities. Yet, as is common in the sphere of nuclear weapons, the mere threat posed by SDI was sufficient to generate significant shockwaves across the Cold War landscape. The sharp increase in American defence spending, of which SDI was a significant proportion, coupled with the USSR's economic problems, convinced many that the Soviet Union was incapable of keeping up in the arms race. As such, particularly after Gorbachev's ascent, SDI became a, not insignificant, 'stick' with which the US 'encouraged' the USSR to agree to arms limitations.

HISTORIOGRAPHY

"There are moments in history when a single dramatic development can galvanise a country into taking action - Sputnik had this effect on the United States in 1957 - and the reaction to SDI in the Soviet Union may have been an example of that."

John Lewis Gaddis
The United States and the End of The Cold War: Implications, Reconsiderations, Provocations

WHERE TO FIND OUT MORE

Way Out There in the Blue: Reagan, Star Wars and the End of the Cold War
Frances FitzGerald

The Strategic Defence Initiative: US Policy and the Soviet Union
Mira Duric

bit.ly/3keZBYV

STRATEGIC DEFENSE INITIATIVE

www.versushistory.com @versushistory

In 1981, US president Ronald Reagan announced a new 1 trillion-dollar defence spending program. As part of, what became known as, the *Reagan Doctrine* the new president decided that the USSR could ill afford a new arms race. Reagan believed that US financial superiority would equal military superiority; in turn, this would destroy the doctrine of Mutually Assured Destruction (M.A.D.).

Part of this military build-up included the SDI, or *Star Wars* – a space and ground-based system capable of intercepting Soviet ICBM's in mid-flight, using methods such as lasers.

ACCORDING TO SOLIDARITY

OVERVIEW

Originating in the Lenin shipyard of the port city of Gdansk, formerly Danzig in Germany, Solidarity was a trade union with a difference. Formed in 1980 and boasting a membership of 10 million in 1981, Solidarity became a powerful force campaigning for social change in Poland by focussing on issues well beyond working conditions. Originally tolerated by the Polish government, this changed in December 1981 when some 10,000 leading activists, including Solidarity's President, Lech Walesa, were rounded up and imprisoned. Solidarity's campaigning continued, however, firstly as an underground movement, but openly after Gorbachev's reforms. Reforms within Poland saw Solidarity running candidates in elections in 1989, winning 260/261 contested seats.

SIGNIFICANCE

Solidarity, and particularly its popularity, stood as stark condemnation of the economic and political situation in 1980's Poland. The experience of Solidarity in 1980 and 1981 allowed it to be at the forefront of the democratic revolution at the end of the decade, seeing Lech Walesa elected President of Poland. Yet, such achievements were only possible with governmental acquiescence. The swift and decisive early repression of Solidarity highlighted the impotent nature of movements, even vastly popular and internationally lauded ones, within the communist systems of the 1980s. In this, Solidarity was more a symbol than an agent of change.

HISTORIOGRAPHY

"Almost all Poles identified and sympathised with Solidarity, including a huge section of the Communist Party. (Even some of Solidarity's opponents in the secret police grew to have a grudging respect for what it stood for and the integrity of its activists)."

Jack M. Bloom
Seeing Through the Eyes of the Polish Revolution

WHERE TO FIND OUT MORE

The Polish Revolution: Solidarity
Timothy Garton Ash

A Covert Action: Reagan, the CIA and the Cold War Battle in Poland
Seth G. Jones

bit.ly/3fv8eec

The blooming of SOLIDARITY

1990
Lech Walesa becomes the first democratically-elected President of Poland.

1989
Constant underground pressure from Solidarity activists reaped rewards: semi-free elections resulted in a Solidarity-led coalition government.

1981+
Despite attempts to oppress Solidarity through martial law, the movement gained international support - both covert and public.

Aug 1980
These workers took the name SOLIDARITY and formed an anti-USSR social movement.

Aug 1980
Led by Walentynowizc and Lech Walesa, the workers went on strike in solidarity with other strikers around Poland.

Aug 1980
Popular crane operator and activist at the Gdansk Shipyard, Anna Walentynowicz, was fired. The workers responded with outrage.

July 1980
The decision by the government of Edward Gierek to freeze wages but increase prices led Polish workers to strike across the country.

1970's
A decade of economic crises galvanised Polish workers against governmental control.

www.versushistory.com

@versushistory

GREMLINS IN THE KREMLIN

OVERVIEW

In 1985 the Soviet Union remained a superpower, but one that was creaking and showing its age. Most obviously its economy was in poor shape. Almost a fifth of spending was devoted to the military in a new arms race, whilst shortages of key goods were common due to the inefficient centrally planned economy. Yet the problems Gorbachev inherited went wider and deeper. In foreign policy the USSR was isolated; there was confrontation with the USA, acrimony with China, tensions with the leadership in satellite states, hostility with Western Europe and an unwinnable war in Afghanistan. Within the USSR itself there was growing dissent, increasing corruption at all levels and question marks lingering over the Chernobyl disaster.

SIGNIFICANCE

There had clearly been a need for reform within the economic and political systems of the USSR for some time, and this had been acknowledged even within the Politburo. However, hardliners had stymied these through much of the 1960s and 70s. As a result, by the 1980s the problems had grown to such a point that radical overhaul and reorganisation of both systems seemed the only option. Yet such an approach carried inherent risks. Far-reaching change, encompassing both the political and economic spheres, would clearly be more difficult to control than incremental, slow paced reform. Despite knowledge of this, the scale of the issues meant Gorbachev felt he had little choice.

HISTORIOGRAPHY

"The daunting challenges that these protracted domestic and foreign policy failures presented were compounded by the fact that the long period of ineffective and incapacitated general secretaries had fractured the total centralized control and power upon which the ideological and systemic foundations of the Soviet structure were based."

Ilya Zemtsov & John Farrar
Gorbachev: The Man and the System

WHERE TO FIND OUT MORE

Armageddon Averted: The Soviet Collapse, 1970-2000
Stephen Kotkin

Memoirs
Mikhail Gorbachev

bit.ly/3osPBmV

GORBACHEV'S WHEEL OF MISFORTUNE

@VERSUS HISTORY   www.VERSUSHISTORY.com

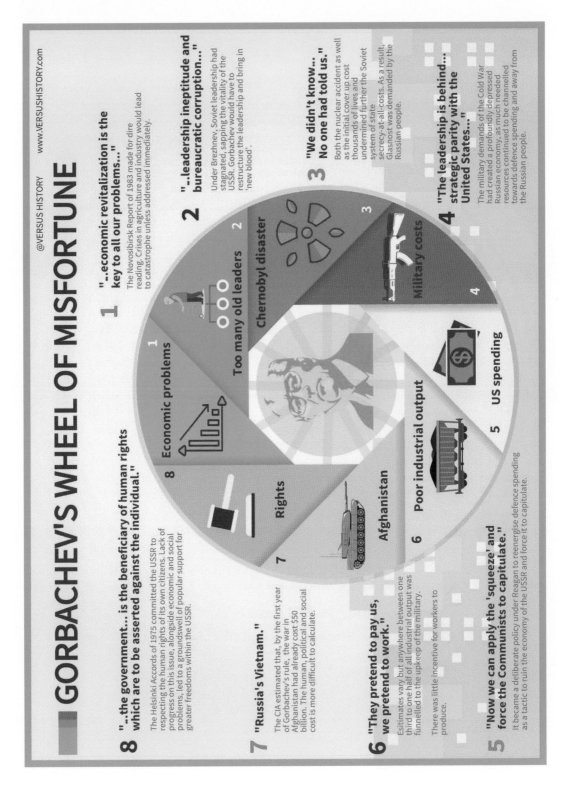

1 "..economic revitalization is the key to all our problems..."

The Novosibirsk Report of 1983 made for dire reading. Crises in agriculture and industry would lead to catastrophe unless addressed immediately.

2 "..leadership ineptitude and bureaucratic corruption..."

Under Brezhnev, Soviet leadership had stagnated, sapping the vitality of the USSR. Gorbachev would have to restructure the leadership and bring in 'new blood'.

3 "We didn't know... No one had told us."

Both the nuclear accident as well as the initial cover up cost thousands of lives and undermined further the Soviet system of state secrecy-at-all-costs. As a result, Glasnost was demanded by the Russian people.

4 "The leadership is behind... strategic parity with the United States..."

The military demands of the Cold War had created a profoundly depressed Russian economy, as much needed resources continued to be channelled towards defence spending and away from the Russian people.

5 "Now we can apply the 'squeeze' and force the Communists to capitulate."

It became a deliberate policy under Reagan to reenergise defence spending as a tactic to ruin the economy of the USSR and force it to capitulate.

6 "They pretend to pay us, we pretend to work."

Estimates vary but anywhere between one third to one half of all industrial output was funnelled to the upkeep of the military.

There was little incentive for workers to produce.

7 "Russia's Vietnam."

The CIA estimated that, by the first year of Gorbachev's rule, the war in Afghanistan had already cost $50 billion. The human, political and social cost is more difficult to calculate.

8 "...the government... is the beneficiary of human rights which are to be asserted against the individual."

The Helsinki Accords of 1975 committed the USSR to respecting the human rights of its own citizens. Lack of progress on this issue, alongside economic and social problems, led to a groundswell of popular support for greater freedoms within the USSR.

Wheel labels: 1 Economic problems · 2 Too many old leaders · Chernobyl disaster · 3 Military costs · 4 US spending · 5 Poor industrial output · 6 Afghanistan · 7 Rights · 8

OPENING PANDORA'S BOX

OVERVIEW

In 1987, Mikhail Gorbachev published a book entitled *Perestroika: A New Thinking for Our Country and the World.* In this book Gorbachev set out the central tenets of what became known as his 'New Thinking'. In his position as General Secretary of the Communist Party, Gorbachev believed that a fundamental re-thinking of Russian international relations, economic principles, ideological imperatives, and security strategies, was required if the USSR was to survive. Make no mistake, the Cold War had helped push the USSR to the brink of collapse; Gorbachev's aims were to preserve the Union and protect socialism. Introducing economic reforms under the umbrella of 'perestroika' alongside political and social reforms in the spirit of 'glasnost', the eighth (and final) leader of the USSR hoped to diffuse the Cold War and improve the lives of ordinary Russians.

SIGNIFICANCE

It hardly needs stating what a break from previous Soviet thinking Gorbachev's new approach was, however, it should also be stated that much of our analysis of his 'New Thinking' comes from our knowledge that the USSR collapsed not long after his reforms were introduced. Although some of the 'blame' for this collapse must rest upon the shoulders of Gorbachev – historians have suggested the reforms were either too radical for the Soviet state to implement or not far-reaching enough to solve her serious problems – the collapse of the Union is far too complex to ascribe its cause to one person. Nonetheless, in a relatively short period of time, Gorbachev was able to heal the Sino-Soviet split, reduce Soviet expenditure on nuclear weapons, increase domestic freedoms, all the while helping to encourage greater friendships with countries of the West. Unfortunately – for Gorbachev – the process of openness and reform created an environment in which the fragile Union could simply no longer exist.

HISTORIOGRAPHY

"…many of the supporters of New Thinking, including Gorbachev, remained incapable of ridding themselves of the ideological baggage accumulated in the seventy years of travel that was intended to lead to a bright future."

Hannes Adomeit
Imperial Overstretch: Germany in Soviet Policy from Stalin to Gorbachev

WHERE TO FIND OUT MORE

New Thinking and New Foreign Policy under Gorbachev
Peter Zwick

Perestroika: A New Thinking for Our Country and the World
Mikhail Gorbachev

bit.ly/31q3z8B

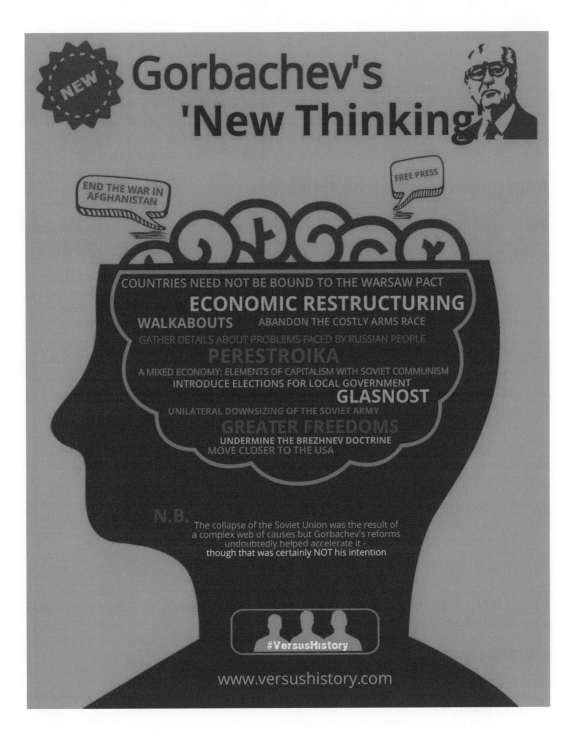

A FAREWELL TO ARMS

OVERVIEW

The destructive force contained in the superpowers' nuclear stockpiles had long been apocalyptic and the threat of their use an imminent concern. The second half of the 1980's, however, would see the prospect of utilisation almost disappear, while stockpiles themselves would begin to shrink. At a series of summit meetings, which could still be fractious, Gorbachev and Reagan (and later, Bush) signed agreements committing to the dismantling of many of their nuclear weapons. The last of these, START, which was signed in 1991, limited each side to 1,600 missiles and 6,000 warheads – a restriction that lasted until 2009.

SIGNIFICANCE

The arms race and the Cold War remained almost inseparable to their respective endings. Nuclear threat supposedly required defensive geopolitical policies, just as the perception of a hostile, malignant superpower enemy apparently necessitated technological, nuclear parity. As such, without agreement in the nuclear sphere, there was no prospect of an end to the Cold War. The ending of the arms race, however, affected geopolitics in many ways beyond reducing US-USSR tensions. Economically, it had a huge positive fiscal impact on both participants, as focus turned to maintenance of stockpiles rather than development of new missiles. Rather than superpower confrontation, nuclear challenges would now primarily entail limiting proliferation while simultaneously restricting the ability of 'rogue states' to nuclearize.

HISTORIOGRAPHY

"A serious meeting of minds occurred as General Secretary and President directed their administrations towards cooperation in reducing the number of nuclear missiles held on land, at sea and in the air... global politics would never be the same again."

Robert Service
The End of the Cold War 1985-91

WHERE TO FIND OUT MORE

The Dead Hand: The Untold Story of the Cold War Arms Race and its Dangerous Legacy
David E. Hoffman

Reagan at Reykjavik: Forty-Eight Hours That Ended the Cold War
Ken Adelman

bit.ly/3gz48TJ

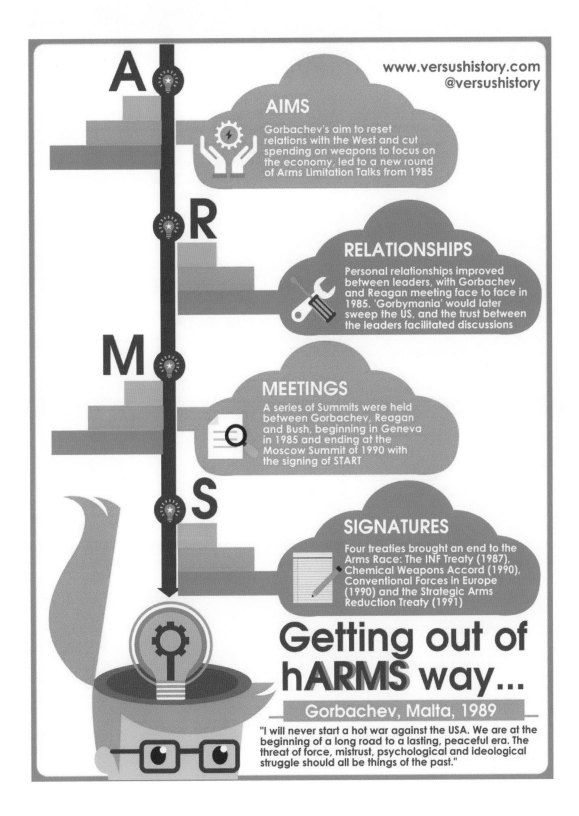

BREAKING DOWN BARRIERS

OVERVIEW

On November 9, 1989, the East German government announced an immediate relaxation on travel restrictions with West Germany. For the first time in 28 years, citizens were to be allowed free passage, with no need for advance notice or permits. This announcement, made in the wake of large scale, escalating protests throughout October and November, meant that the most poignant symbol of Cold War Europe lost its 'raison d'etre'. Following the declaration, crowds gathered at checkpoints to welcome East Berliners to the West, but it was images of those at the wall itself, celebrating and dismantling it with handheld tools which would go around the world.

SIGNIFICANCE

The physical demolition of the wall made little difference to East-West travel. Instead, this occurred at border crossings across Berlin (where 1 million a day took advantage to temporarily cross to the West), Germany and much of Europe. However, the destruction of the Wall via the power of mass protest, catalysed the revolutions already underway in East Germany and throughout the satellite states. The Wall's fall ensured that Berlin would, as it had through the whole Cold War, stand as a microcosm of wider developments. It was a combination of the Wall's visual symbolism and Berlin's historic role as the crux of Cold War tensions, which meant that, despite similar revolutions occurring across Eastern Europe, it was East Germany's that would be the most televised and ingrained in the West's consciousness.

HISTORIOGRAPHY

"Although the Wall came down on November 9, the real end of Soviet domination in Eastern Europe occurred far less dramatically in a secret meeting months before, where Gorbachev told his socialist counterparts that the Kremlin would never again crush Eastern European reformers with force."

Jeffrey A. Engel
The Fall of the Berlin Wall: The Revolutionary Legacy of 1989

WHERE TO FIND OUT MORE

1989: The Year that Changed the World: The Untold Story Behind the Fall of the Berlin Wall
Michael Meyer

Collapse: The Accidental Opening of the Berlin Wall
Mary Sarotte

bit.ly/3ketEzY

1989

The Collapse of the
BERLIN WALL

Though the culmination of a complex web of causes, the events of November 9th, 1989 moved so swiftly that they caught most people off guard – particularly the leaders and people of East Germany. Before people could understand what was really happening, the Berlin Wall was forever a memory. Albeit an unpleasant one.

4th November, half a million people protested in East Berlin over travel restrictions

Without clear instructions, and completely outnumbered, the border guards eventually opened all checkpoints at 10.45pm

The East German Politburo redrafted restrictions to allow applications for travel abroad

Party leader, Günter Schabowski, mistakenly announced that immediate travel between East and West Berlin was permissable

News of the announcement spread like wildfire and thousands of East Berliners crowded the border

On November 9th, life in Germany moved VERY fast

www.versushistory.com
@versushistory

A HOUSE IN DISORDER

OVERVIEW

When the end of the USSR came, it was swift and surprising in nature. Over the course of just a few days, the wall came down and the Union began to falter. Despite the speed at which events transpired in 1989, the disintegration of a communist Russia that had existed since 1917, had very deep roots. The USSR had long been buckling under the economic strain of the Cold War – a strain that had been exacerbated by her failed adventurism in Afghanistan. Ruled by an increasingly weak and aging Party that was either politically unwilling, or acutely unable, to address the inefficiency of a monolithic centralised government and economy, the people of the USSR and her satellite states began calling for reform. Nationalist uprisings in places such as Tbilisi, as well as growing opposition to Soviet control in Eastern Europe, began to test the Kremlin's control. With the broad failure of Gorbachev's reforms to address the hardships faced by those within and without the borders of the USSR, long-term problems coupled with the possibility of change-through-protest (encouraged by Glasnost), helped bring down the communist regime.

SIGNIFICANCE

Just how important to the collapse of the Soviet Union these internal issues and external pressures were, is a matter of some debate. Some historians, such as Aleksei Filitov and Rosemary Williams, see the end of the Cold War and the collapse of the USSR as almost entirely separate 'ends', where one (the end of the Cold War) helped lead to the other (Soviet disintegration). Regardless of whether these two 'ends' are differentiated or conflated, the political, social and economic instability of the USSR played a profound role in the collapse of communist Russia. When coupled to Gorbachev's attempts at reform – which simultaneously frustrated and encouraged the peoples of Russia and the Eastern Bloc – one is left with the obvious conclusion: though collapse, when it came, was swift, it was long in the making.

HISTORIOGRAPHY

"...all these thoughts and emotions (of the Russian people about their government)...were displaced by deep disappointment with the leadership and its socio-political model."

Aleksei Filitov and Rosemary Williams
The End of the Cold War and the Dissolution of the USSR

WHERE TO FIND OUT MORE

Revisiting the Collapse of the USSR
David R. Marples

The Third World and the Dissolution of the USSR
Mark Webber

bit.ly/3IqeTBm

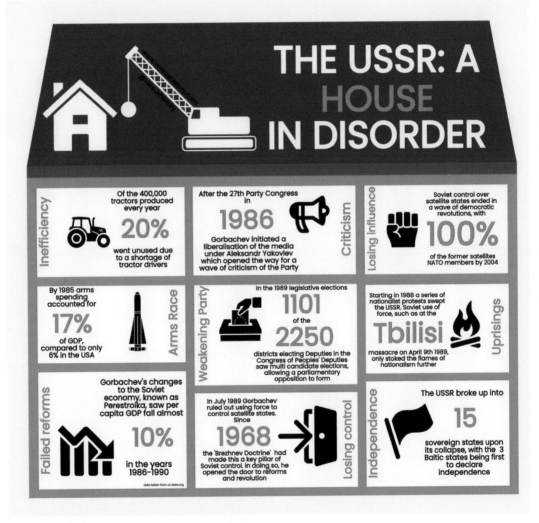

THE USSR: A HOUSE IN DISORDER

Inefficiency

Of the 400,000 tractors produced every year

20%

went unused due to a shortage of tractor drivers

Criticism

After the 27th Party Congress in

1986

Gorbachev initiated a liberalisation of the media under Aleksandr Yakovlev which opened the way for a wave of criticism of the Party

Losing influence

Soviet control over satellite states ended in a wave of democratic revolutions, with

100%

of the former satellites NATO members by 2004

Arms Race

By 1985 arms spending accounted for

17%

of GDP, compared to only 6% in the USA

Weakening Party

In the 1989 legislative elections

1101

of the

2250

districts electing Deputies in the Congress of Peoples' Deputies saw multi candidate elections, allowing a parliamentary opposition to form

Uprisings

Starting in 1988 a series of nationalist protests swept the USSR. Soviet use of force, such as at the

Tbilisi

massacre on April 9th 1989, only stoked the flames of nationalism further

Failed reforms

Gorbachev's changes to the Soviet economy, known as Perestroika, saw per capita GDP fall almost

10%

in the years 1986–1990

data taken from un.data.org

Losing control

In July 1989 Gorbachev ruled out using force to control satellite states. Since

1968

the 'Brezhnev Doctrine' had made this a key pillar of Soviet control. In doing so, he opened the door to reforms and revolution

Independence

The USSR broke up into

15

sovereign states upon its collapse, with the 3 Baltic states being first to declare independence

GAME OVER

OVERVIEW

On December 25, 1991 Mikhail Gorbachev resigned his position as President of the Soviet Union. The very next day, the Supreme Soviet of the Soviet Union – the highest institution of state power – dissolved the USSR with a vote. For 74 years history's first communist nation helped shape the world in ways unimaginable to those Bolsheviks that overthrew the Provisional Government in October 1917. The Cold War had ended ostensibly when the Berlin Wall came down, but the Soviet Union continued for a further two years. Through a complex mix of causation: from the demands of the Cold War to the promising but largely unsuccessful reforms of Gorbachev, from the crumbling economy to the nationalist demands of those within the Eastern Bloc, the USSR found itself simply unable to hold its vast eastern hegemony together.

SIGNIFICANCE

When the Soviet Union collapsed, the world became a unipolar one: only the USA remained as a fully-fledged superpower. As the disintegration of the Union gathered pace, securing the country's vast nuclear arsenal became one of the primary concerns of the international community. Where were all of the nuclear weapons? Who legally controlled them now? How could they be secured without sufficient funds? Less dangerous but no less dramatic, sports teams that had once competed under the banner of the USSR now had to determine their own sporting future. With the Winter Olympics just around the corner, decisions had to be made quickly. The economic bonds between the USSR and the Eastern Bloc that had largely managed to paper over cracks, once removed, led to an economic depression in the former satellite states to rival the Great Depression of the 1930's. With the USSR no more and the hammer and sickle flag lowered for the final time over the Kremlin on December 25th, Boris Yeltsin became the president of the new Russian Federation, ushering in a new era of Russian and global history.

HISTORIOGRAPHY

"The end of the Soviet Union has been a matter of such tremendous importance that no country of the world has been able to quarantine itself from its all pervasive impact."

Bipattaran Ghosh
The Collapse of the Soviet Union: Some Major Implications

WHERE TO FIND OUT MORE

Reflections on Collapse of USSR
Yamini Kumar

Nationalism and the Collapse of Soviet Communism
Mark R. Beissinger

bit.ly/30uLwyJ

The Historical Record

USSR COLLAPSES!

"Is this the end of History?"

Local bystander, Mr F. Fukuyama

A CATALYST?

As Gorbachev loosened Soviet control over the countries of Eastern Europe, democratic movements created a momentum that ultimately resulted in the fall of the Berlin Wall in 1989. These movements did not end with wall's collapse.

ELECTIONS!

Gorbachev allowed for multi-party elections and the creation of a presidency in Russia. This democratisation destabilised Communist control of Russia and created a schism between conservative communists and those looking to liberalise the country.

WITHDRAWAL!

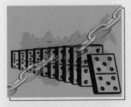

Gorbachev announced the withdrawal of the Red Army from East Germany and agreed to German reunification. This was good for his international prestige but caused major problems for the survival of the USSR.

ATTEMPTED COUP!

With the collapse of Communist regimes in Eastern Europe stimulating demands for independence from the Caucasus and Baltic states, hardline Communists attempted a coup against Gorbachev in August 1991.

FALLING DOMINOES!

Despite the failure of the coup, Gorbachev resigned from what was left of the USSR on December 25th December 1991. He was the 11th and final leader of Communist Russia. Before resigning, he ordered the dissolution of the Central Committee of the Communist Party.

HAMMER AND SICKLE LOWERS FOREVER

The hammer and sickle flag, so well known throughout the twentieth century world, is lowered over the Kremlin for the last time on December 25th, 1991.

WWW.VERSUSHISTORY.COM @VERSUSHISTORY

A COLD INHERITANCE

The significance of any event, issue, individual or group in history is so inevitably bound up with an interpretation of the *degree* to which they have generated an impact or influence. Since the Cold War is comprised of a near infinite number of these events, issues, individuals, and groups – spanning at least the period of 1945-89 – the challenge that historians face in determining any form of impact or influence is complex, to say the least. Even attempting to single out *one* significant legacy of the Cold War is fraught with difficulty.

The point is this: the Cold War shaped and reshaped the world in so many ways and with so many outcomes, that doing them all justice here would be impossible. Historians – the readers of this book – must choose their own strands of the Cold War to examine and then determine the significance of these strands based upon clear evaluative metrics. Perhaps the manipulation of so-called 'Third World' countries in Africa, Asia and Latin America by the USSR and US – leaving behind indelible hallmarks of superpower exploitation – should be considered an enduring legacy. Maybe the technology we enjoy today, driven by the 'arms race' and the 'space race', deserves attention when discussing Cold War endowments to history. No matter what series of strands are selected as 'worthy' of evaluation, there a few key questions that need to be answered in the process: 1) Why have these strands been selected for study? 2) By what metrics will *significance* be measured? 3) Against which other strands can a relative comparison of importance be made?

An interesting way of examining the legacy of the Cold War might be to determine the importance of its *absence*. For example, one could explain that, since the Cold War dominated the geo-political international environment for nearly fifty years, its absence as of 1989 is what created the greatest changes in the historical record. How might something *ceasing* to exist affect history, and therefore its legacy? To complicate matters even further, how far into the future does the legacy of the Cold war stretch? When do the impacts of any event cease to be significant? In short, does a legacy ever truly end, or is it like Günter Grass said in his book *Crabwalk:* "It doesn't end. Never will it end".

WHERE TO FIND OUT MORE

After Victory: Institutions, Strategic Restraint, and the Rebuilding of Order after Major Wars
G. John Ikenberry

Brain Warfare: The Covert Sphere, Terrorism, and the Legacy of the Cold War
Timothy Melley

Legacy of the Cold War in Indochina
Townsend Hoopes

Ruins of the Cold War
Yuliya Komska

bit.ly/39XA9IX

THE LEGACY OF THE COLD WAR

GLOBAL LEGACY:

A UNIPOLAR WORLD
The end of the Cold War essentially left the world with only one economic, political and military superpower. Consequently, the US was able to create a global hegemony in everything from culture to finance.

USSR SHATTERED
The collapse of the Soviet Union created an entirely new map of Eurasia. The geo-political, economic, national, and cultural consequences of this are near immeasurable in their impact and complexity.

NUCLEAR WAR
The world had become accustomed to the ever-present threat of nuclear annihilation. With the collapse of the USSR there was now the threat that their unsecured nuclear weapons could fall into the 'wrong hands'.

MILITARY LEGACY:

39,000
POTENTIALLY UNSECURED NUCLEAR WEAPONS

Government scientists from the US and the USSR cooperated to ensure the security of nuclear nuclear material belonging to the former Soviet Union.

1.5 million
AMERICAN TROOPS IN 117 COUNTRIES IN 1989

During the Cold War, the USA spread its military influence around the world. Many of these military alliances continued after the Cold War was over.

Millions of soldiers and civilians died during the 'proxy wars' fought by the two superpowers.

THE 'THIRD WORLD' LEGACY

With both superpowers apparently accepting of the status quo in Cold War Europe, they began to look for ways to dominate countries not already within their spheres of influence. The 'First World' was the term used to describe the US and her European allies; the 'Second World' described the USSR and her allies. Countries that had not aligned themselves in the Cold War - the so-called 'Third World' - became the new battleground for the USSR and USA. With often terrible consequences.

Between 1946-1960 thirty seven new nations emerged out of imperial bondage. The USSR & the USA would attempt to either court or destroy each one of these. Neutrality was not tolerated by either superpower.

Many 'Third World' nations, such as those in the Middle East, held valuable resources. Competition to control and exploit these resources often led to relationships that drew these nations into the Cold War. Often at great, and sometimes deadly, cost.

Communism was attractive to poorer states looking to throw off the shackles of capitalism. The Communist Bloc encouraged revolutionary wars within the 'Third World' that were usually countered by the US - with often tragic consequences.

The US & USSR would offer aid and assistance to countries, but these offers came with strings attached. A country might access greater levels of trade and business, but they were often saddled with debt and exploited by foreign industries.

#VersusHistory

@VERSUSHISTORY
WWW.VERSUSHISTORY.COM

THE KEY...

Studying any period of history is a challenge. Studying a period of history that involves a particular nomenclature – system of language – is an even greater challenge. Studying a period of history that has a particular nomenclature which is occasionally in an *unfamiliar language*, is the greatest challenge. If the language of the Cold War, including Russian, is unfamiliar to you – the reader – then the following few pages might help you navigate some of the key words and terms that are often used in the study of this period. This is not an exhaustive glossary – that would require a book in itself – but it will give the reader a sample of terminology that is specific to this period that can be used to unlock greater understanding.

The infographic opposite can be accessed using the QR Code/URL below, whilst the glossary in the following pages can be downloaded using the QR Code/URL on the infographic itself. Go unlock your understanding.

bit.ly/3fqbzve

Appeasement

The policy of making concessions to aggressive leaders in the hope that it will ultimately make them less aggressive. This policy had been followed by Britain and France towards Hitler before the outbreak of World War Two. It was seen as a failure because it failed to stop Nazi expansion.

As a result, any form of appeasement during the Cold War was viewed negatively.

Bizonia

The name given to the British and US zones of Germany once they merged in 1947.

Brinkmanship

A strategy of increasing risk and threat followed by leaders in the hope that the opposition will back down. The Cuban Missile Crisis is often viewed as an example of brinkmanship.

Carter Doctrine

The foreign policy followed by President Jimmy Carter after the Soviet Invasion of Afghanistan and the Iranian Revolution of 1979. Carter promised to protect America's sphere of influence in the Persian Gulf using military force, if necessary.

www.versushistory.com
@versushistory

Arms Race

The contest between the USA and USSR to develop the most advanced weaponry and in the greatest number, particularly in the nuclear field.

Brezhnev Doctrine

Set of policies announced by Soviet leader Leonid Brezhnev in 1968, which intimated that the USSR had a right and duty to intervene wherever Communism was under threat, even within other sovereign nations.

Capitalism

The economic system used in the USA and the 'West'. Within this system business and industry is mostly controlled by private individuals to make a profit. By extension it also came to imply a political system in which leaders are chosen through democratic elections.

Checkpoint Charlie

The name given to the most prominent border crossing in the Berlin Wall between East and West Berlin. It was often the scene of confrontation and posturing between the USSR and the Allies.

COMECON

The Council of Mutual Assistance evolved out of the Molotov Plan, which was the equivalent of the Marshall Plan, but organised by the USSR. It created an economic group consisting of the USSR and the socialist satellite states of Eastern Europe.

COMINFORM

The Communist Information Bureau existed between the years 1947-56 and was designed, in part, to ensure uniformity and compliance between the countries of the Eastern Bloc.

COMINTERN

Ending in 1943, the Communist International was an organisation headquartered in Moscow that sought to encourage and spread communism around the world.

Communism

The economic and political system used in the USSR and Eastern Europe during the Cold War. Within this system industry is centrally controlled and directed by the state, while wealth is collectively rather than individually owned. Politically, Communism is characterised by one party control, with no democratic route to changing this.

Containment

A policy adopted by the USA, as part of the Truman Doctrine, which sought to stop Communism from expanding into new states or regions.

Détente

French word denoting a 'relaxation of tensions'. A period of time, from the mid 1960s until the late 1970s, in which relations between the superpowers were less tense and a series of agreements were made.

Domino Theory

A theory contending that, should communism rise in one country, it would then likely spread to its neighbouring countries. The domino theory was used as justification for the American containment policy being pursued in Asia.

Espionage

The practice of using covert/secret methods to undermine governments of other countries. These methods can range from spying to assassination.

www.versushistory.com
@versushistory

Federal Republic of Germany

The official title of West Germany between the years 1949-1990.

General Secretary

The highest ranking position within a Communist Party (sometimes called the First Secretary). In most communist states, including the USSR, this would also be the key decision maker and leader.

German Democratic Republic

The official title of East Germany between the years 1949-1990.

Glasnost

Russian word meaning 'openness' that was used to describe a series of reforms applied by Gorbachev that were designed to encourage greater democratic freedoms within the USSR.

Grand Alliance

The name given to the World War Two alliance between the USSR, Britain, and the US.

ICBM

Intercontinental Ballistic Missile. A missile type, capable of flying over c.5,500km, which can be precision-guided to a target location. Capable of carrying at least one nuclear warhead.

Iron Curtain

A figurative term used to illustrate the division of Europe between the communist East and capitalist West. The 'curtain' was an imaginary line which ran North-South along the borders dividing the two halves of Europe.

Kremlin

The Kremlin is often used to refer to the seat of executive government within the Soviet Union. It is essentially the Soviet equivalent of the White House in Washington.

www.versushistory.com
@versushistory

Long Telegram

A diplomatic cable sent by the US Ambassador in Moscow - George Kennan - to the US State Department in 1946. It outlined George Kennan's interpretation of Soviet foreign policy and offered advice as to how the US should approach it. This helped form the basis of the Truman Doctrine and America's containment policy.

MAD

Mutually Assured Destruction. The concept that were one side to attack the other, they would themselves endure massive, catastrophic nuclear retaliation. This idea was seen to bring stability to the Cold War as it acted as a strong deterrent.

Madman Theory

This was a strategy utilised by President Nixon that hoped to demonstrate to the USSR and China that he was unstable and may use nuclear weapons against them. Mixed signals, deliberate misinformation, and apparently 'unusual behaviour' helped promulgate the strategy.

Marshall Plan

European Recovery Program. A program developed by the USA as a means to support the economies of Europe. By investing over $18 billion, which came with limitations on how it could be used, the Marshall Plan was intended to stop favourable conditions for Communism developing in Europe.

McCarthyism

A generic term used to refer to making accusations without evidence. It derived its name from Senator Joseph McCarthy who made allegations that there were hundreds of communists within the US State Department. These accusations helped fuel the 'Red Scare' and stoke anti-communist hysteria in the USA.

Minuteman

A US ICBM, the Minuteman was the first to be powered by solid fuel and therefore able to be kept ready for launch at all times.

Missile Gap

A belief, held by the USA in the late 1950s, that the Soviet Union possessed more numerous and more powerful missiles than they did.

MIRV

Multiple Independently Targetable Reentry Vehicle. Missiles capable of carrying multiple nuclear warheads. These could be individually targeted to different sites, allowing one missile to bring destruction to a variety of locations.

www.versushistory.com
@versushistory

Molotov Plan

The precursor to COMECON (see above).

Mujahideen

Term used to describe Islamist fighters seeking to remove the communist government of Afghanistan as well as the USSR from Afghan soil, in the late 1970s and 1980s.

NATO

North Atlantic Treaty Organisation. Organisation bringing together the USA and most of the Western powers in a mutual defence pact. Formed in 1949, it originally consisted of 12 nations but, as of 2020, has expanded to 30 member states. Despite its stated defensive aims, it was seen by the USSR as an expansive aggressive movement.

NAM

Non Aligned Movement. Organisation, officially founded in 1961, which comprises nations who do not want to be aligned with any power 'blocs'. During the Cold War they sought to act independently of the USA and USSR.

NORAD

North American Aerospace Defense Command. Organisation, formed in 1958, which combines US and Canadian resources to coordinate protection of North America's airspace.

Novikov Telegram

A communication from the USSR's ambassador in Washington - Nikolai Novikov - back to the USSR which outlined the potential for the USA to seek global dominance in opposition to the USSR.

Nuclear Deterrence

The principle that possession of nuclear weapons means other states are unlikely to attack. A cornerstone of superpower thought in the Cold War.

Ostpolitik

Eastern Policy. A policy adopted by West Germany under the influence of Willy Brand, to develop closer ties and better relations with Eastern Europe, but particularly East Germany.

www.versushistory.com
@versushistory

Perestroika

Restructuring. A catch-all term for a series of reforms, both economic and political, introduced by Mikhail Gorbachev within the USSR in the late 1980s.

Ping Pong Diplomacy

Nickname given to attempts to improve relations between the USA and Communist China in the early 1970s. Supposedly instigated by a chance meeting at the Table Tennis World Championships.

Politburo

Political Bureau of the Central Committee of the Communist Party. A shortened term used to refer to the most powerful decision-making body within the USSR.

Prague Spring

A period of time in 1968 when reforms, under the direction of Alexander Dubček, were implemented in Czechoslovakia. It was ended by the Warsaw Pact invasion in August.

Proxy War

A war fought between two factions, parties or countries in which each side is supported by a different, more powerful nation or group.

Reagan Doctrine

A term used to describe the foreign policy goal, adopted by President Reagan, of supporting anti-communist insurgents around the world in an attempt to rollback Communism.

Red Army

The army of the Soviet Union

Rollback

A description of intermittent US policy which sought to not just contain, but proactively shrink the areas of the world under communist control. Examples are US actions in the Korean War, the Bay of Pigs invasion and actions taken to support anti-communist insurgencies.

Rollback, when applied, meant the policy of containment had to be 'paused'.

www.versushistory.com
@versushistory

SALT

Strategic Arms Limitation Talks. Two conferences between the US and USSR that sought to limit the construction and proliferation of nuclear weapons.

Satellite States

A nickname given to the communist states of Eastern Europe within Moscow's 'sphere of influence'. Despite having their own governments, they were essentially controlled from Moscow.

SDI

Strategic Defense Initiative. A missile defense system, announced by Ronald Reagan in 1982, which sought to neutralise the threat of the USSR's nuclear arsenal. Also known as 'Star Wars.

Secret Speech

A secret address given by Soviet Premier Nikita Khrushchev to the Congress of Soviets in 1956. The speech denounced Stalinism and the brutality of his regime.

Sino-Soviet Split

A term used to describe the political and diplomatic divergence of the Soviet Union and China, particularly in the late 1960s. This split led to some military conflict between the two powers and provided an opportunity for the US to build, temporarily, closer relationships with both countries.

SLBM

Submarine Launched Ballistic Missile. Seen as a particularly potent nuclear defence due to the difficulty of locating submarines; this meant a preemptive land-based nuclear strike was impossible.

Solidarnosc

Solidarity. A trade union in Poland, later a political party, founded in 1980 which was independent and sought to implement a series of reforms within communist Poland.

Soviet Bloc

A term used to describe the states aligned with the Soviet Union during the Cold War.

www.versushistory.com
@versushistory

Space Race

A contest between both the USA and the USSR to be first to achieve significant milestones in space for either propaganda value or military potential.

Sputnik

The first man-made satellite, launched in 1957 by the Soviet Union. Translated as 'fellow-traveller'.

START

Strategic Arms Reduction Talks. A series of talks beginning in 1982 between the USA and USSR, focussed on reducing their nuclear arsenals. Culminated in the signing of an arms control treaty (START I) in 1991.

Superpower

A term used to describe both the USA and USSR during the Cold War. It connotes the idea that the nation is able to exert global influence and possesses immense power.

Thaw

Using the metaphor of ice melting to denote a period during which relations between the USA and USSR eased and became less tense.

Trizonia

The name given to the British, US and French zones of Germany once they merged in 1949.

Truman Doctrine

A policy adopted by the USA after it was announced by President Truman in 1947. It outlined the USA's commitment to supporting democratic nations and peoples anywhere in the world under threat from communism. In practice this meant containing communism and stopping its spread.

Tsar Bomba

The nickname given by the West to a bomb detonated by the USSR in 1961. This Hydrogen bomb was the largest ever to have been exploded.

www.versushistory.com
@versushistory

U2

A spy plane developed by the USA with the ability to fly to an altitude of 70,000 feet, supposedly above the range of defences. Carried a high resolution camera for surveillance.

United Nations

A multilateral organisation formed in 1945 that attempted, much like the League of Nations, to solve international disputes and encourage global peace and prosperity. Still in existence today.

USSR

Union of Socialist Soviet Republics. The official name of the Soviet Union. The USSR was supposedly a collection of different republics, although in practice they were all centrally run from Moscow.

Việt Cộng

Colloquial term derived from contracting the name Việt Nam Cộng-sản. Used pejoratively by the government of South Vietnam and the US to refer to the Liberation Army of South Vietnam, which was attempting to overthrow the government from within the south.

Việt Minh

The shortened name for the Việt Nam Độc Lập Đồng Minh Hội, which was a nationalist liberation army led by Ho Chi Minh that fought to liberate Vietnam from foreign interference.

War of Ideas

The Cold War could be said to be a 'war of ideas' at its heart. The USA and the USSR sought to promote their core ways of life abroad through strategic planning and winning of the 'hearts and minds' of people.

Warsaw Pact

A counterpoint to NATO, the Warsaw Pact was an organisation formed in 1955 that served as a defensive pact between the communist states of Eastern Europe. It would, however, be used against one of its members - Czechoslovakia - in 1968.

Western Bloc

A term used to describe the states aligned with the United States during the Cold War.

www.versushistory.com
@versushistory

THE KEY...TO UNDERSTANDING THE COLD WAR

Appeasement

The policy of making concessions to aggressive leaders in the hope that it will ultimately make them less aggressive. This policy had been followed by Britain and France towards Hitler before the outbreak of World War Two. It was seen as a failure because it failed to stop Nazi expansion. As a result, any form of appeasement during the Cold War was viewed negatively.

Arms Race

The contest between the USA and USSR to develop the most advanced weaponry and in the greatest number, particularly in the nuclear field.

Bizonia

The name given to the British and US zones of Germany once they merged in 1947.

Brezhnev Doctrine

An idea, announced by Soviet leader Leonid Brezhnev in 1968, which intimated that the USSR had a right and duty to intervene wherever communism was under threat, even within other sovereign nations.

Brinkmanship

A strategy of increasing risk and threat followed by leaders in the hope that the opposition will back down. The Cuban Missile Crisis is often viewed as an example of brinkmanship.

Capitalism

The economic system used in the USA and the 'West'. Within this system business and industry is mostly controlled by private individuals to make a profit. By extension it also came to imply a political system in which leaders are chosen through democratic elections.

Carter Doctrine

The foreign policy followed by President Jimmy Carter after the Soviet Invasion of Afghanistan and the Iranian Revolution of 1979. Carter promised to protect America's sphere of influence in the Persian Gulf using military force, if necessary.

Checkpoint Charlie

The name given to the most prominent border crossing in the Berlin Wall between East and West Berlin. It was often the scene of confrontation and posturing between the USSR and the Allies.

COMECON

The Council of Mutual Assistance evolved out of the Molotov Plan, which was the equivalent of the Marshall Plan, but organised by the USSR. It created an economic group consisting of the USSR and the socialist satellite states of Eastern Europe.

COMINFORM

The Communist Information Bureau existed between the years 1947-56 and was designed, in part, to ensure uniformity and compliance between the countries of the Eastern Bloc.

COMINTERN
Ending in 1943, the Communist International was an organisation headquartered in Moscow that sought to encourage and spread communism around the world.

Communism
The economic and political system used in the USSR and Eastern Europe during the Cold War. Within this system industry is centrally controlled and directed by the state, while wealth is collectively rather than individually owned. Politically, communism is characterised by one party control, with no democratic route to changing this.

Containment
A policy adopted by the USA, as part of the Truman Doctrine, which sought to stop communism from expanding into new states or regions.

Détente
French word denoting a 'relaxation of tensions'. A period of time, from the mid-1960s until the late 1970s, in which relations between the superpowers were less tense and a series of agreements were made.

Domino Theory
A theory contending that, should communism rise in one country, it would then likely spread to its neighbouring countries. The domino theory was used as justification for the American containment policy being pursued in Asia.

Espionage
The practice of using covert/secret methods to undermine governments of other countries. These methods can range from spying to assassination.

Federal Republic of Germany
The official title of West Germany between the years 1949-1990.

General Secretary
The highest ranking position within a Communist Party (sometimes called the First Secretary). In most communist states, including the USSR, this would also be the key decision maker and leader.

German Democratic Republic
The official title of East Germany between the years 1949-1990.

Glasnost
Russian word meaning 'openness' that was used to describe a series of reforms applied by Gorbachev that were designed to encourage greater democratic freedoms within the USSR.

Grand Alliance
The name given to the World War Two alliance between the USSR, Britain, and the US.

ICBM

Intercontinental Ballistic Missile. A missile type, capable of flying over c.5,500km, which can be precision-guided to a target location. Capable of carrying at least one nuclear warhead.

Iron Curtain

A figurative term used to illustrate the division of Europe between the communist East and capitalist West. The 'curtain' was an imaginary line which ran North–South along the borders dividing the two halves of Europe.

Kremlin

The Kremlin is often used to refer to the seat of executive government within the Soviet Union. It is essentially the Soviet equivalent of the White House in Washington.

Long Telegram

A diplomatic cable sent by the US Ambassador in Moscow – George Kennan – to the US State Department in 1946. It outlined George Kennan's interpretation of Soviet foreign policy and offered advice as to how the US should approach it. This helped form the basis of the Truman Doctrine and America's containment policy.

MAD

Mutually Assured Destruction. The concept that, were one side to attack the other, they would themselves endure massive, catastrophic nuclear retaliation. This idea was seen to bring stability to the Cold War as it acted as a strong deterrent.

Madman Theory

This was a strategy utilised by President Nixon that hoped to demonstrate to the USSR and China that he was unstable and may use nuclear weapons against them. Mixed signals, deliberate misinformation, and apparently 'unusual behaviour' helped promulgate the strategy.

Marshall Plan

European Recovery Program. A program developed by the USA as a means to support the economies of Europe. By investing over $18 billion, which came with limitations on how it could be used, the Marshall Plan was intended to stop favourable conditions for communism developing in Europe.

McCarthyism

A generic term used to refer to making accusations without evidence. It derived its name from Senator Joseph McCarthy who made allegations that there were hundreds of communists within the US State Department. These accusations helped fuel the 'Red Scare' and stoke anti-communist hysteria in the USA.

Minuteman

A US ICBM, the Minuteman was the first to be powered by solid fuel and therefore able to be kept ready for launch at all times.

Missile Gap
A belief, held by the USA in the late 1950s, that the Soviet Union possessed more numerous and more powerful missiles than they did.

MIRV
Multiple Independently Targetable Reentry Vehicle. Missiles capable of carrying multiple nuclear warheads. These could be individually targeted to different sites, allowing one missile to bring destruction to a variety of locations.

Molotov Plan
The precursor to COMECON (see above).

Mujahideen
Term used to describe Islamist fighters seeking to remove the communist government of Afghanistan as well as the USSR from Afghan soil, in the late 1970s and 1980s.

NATO
North Atlantic Treaty Organisation. Organisation bringing together the USA and most of the Western powers in a mutual defence pact. Formed in 1949, it originally consisted of 12 nations but, as of 2020, has expanded to 30 member states. Despite its stated defensive aims, it was seen by the USSR as an expansive aggressive movement.

NAM
Non Aligned Movement. Organisation, officially founded in 1961, which comprises nations who do not want to be aligned with any power 'blocs'. During the Cold War they sought to act independently of the USA and USSR.

NORAD
North American Aerospace Defense Command. Organisation, formed in 1958, which combines US and Canadian resources to coordinate protection of North America's airspace.

Novikov Telegram
A communication from the USSR's ambassador in Washington - Nikolai Novikov - back to the USSR which outlined the potential for the USA to seek global dominance in opposition to the USSR.

Nuclear Deterrence
The principle that possession of nuclear weapons means other states are unlikely to attack. A cornerstone of superpower thought in the Cold War.

Ostpolitik
Eastern Policy. A policy adopted by West Germany under the influence of Willy Brand, to develop closer ties and better relations with Eastern Europe, but particularly East Germany.

Perestroika
Restructuring. A catch-all term for a series of reforms, both economic and political, introduced by Mikhail Gorbachev within the USSR in the late 1980s.

Ping Pong Diplomacy
Nickname given to attempts to improve relations between the USA and communist China in the early 1970s. Supposedly instigated by a chance meeting at the Table Tennis World Championships.

Politburo
Political Bureau of the Central Committee of the Communist Party. A shortened term used to refer to the most powerful decision-making body within the USSR.

Prague Spring
A period of time in 1968 when reforms, under the direction of Alexander Dubcek, were implemented in Czechoslovakia. It was ended by the Warsaw Pact invasion in August.

Proxy War
A war fought between two factions, parties or countries in which each side is supported by a different, more powerful nation or group.

Reagan Doctrine
A term used to describe the foreign policy goal, adopted by President Reagan, of supporting anti-communist insurgents around the world in an attempt to rollback communism.

Red Army
The army of the Soviet Union

Rollback
A description of intermittent US policy which sought to not just contain, but proactively shrink the areas of the world under communist control. Examples are US actions in the Korean War, the Bay of Pigs invasion and actions taken to support anti-communist insurgencies. Rollback, when applied, meant the policy of containment had to be 'paused'.

SALT
Strategic Arms Limitation Talks. Two conferences between the US and USSR that sought to limit the construction and proliferation of nuclear weapons.

Satellite States
A nickname given to the communist states of Eastern Europe within Moscow's 'sphere of influence'. Despite having their own governments, they were essentially controlled from Moscow.

SDI
Strategic Defense Initiative. A missile defense system, announced by Ronald Reagan in 1982, which sought to neutralise the threat of the USSR's nuclear arsenal. Also known as 'Star Wars.

Secret Speech
A secret address given by Soviet Premier Nikita Khrushchev to the Congress of Soviets in 1956. The speech denounced Stalinism and the brutality of his regime.

Sino-Soviet Split
A term used to describe the political and diplomatic divergence of the Soviet Union and China, particularly in the late 1960s. This split led to some military conflict between the two powers and provided an opportunity for the US to build, temporarily, closer relationships with both countries.

SLBM
Submarine Launched Ballistic Missile. Seen as a particularly potent nuclear defence due to the difficulty of locating submarines; this meant a preemptive land-based nuclear strike was impossible.

Solidarnosc
Solidarity. A trade union in Poland, later a political party, founded in 1980 which was independent and sought to implement a series of reforms within communist Poland.

Soviet Bloc
A term used to describe the states aligned with the Soviet Union during the Cold War.

Space Race
A contest between both the USA and the USSR to be first to achieve significant milestones in space for either propaganda value or military potential.

Sputnik
The first man-made satellite, launched in 1957 by the Soviet Union. Translated as 'fellow-traveller'.

START
Strategic Arms Reduction Talks. A series of talks beginning in 1982 between the USA and USSR, focussed on reducing their nuclear arsenals. Culminated in the signing of an arms control treaty (START I) in 1991.

Superpower
A term used to describe both the USA and USSR during the Cold War. It connotes the idea that the nation is able to exert global influence and possesses immense power.

Thaw
Using the metaphor of ice melting to denote a period during which relations between the USA and USSR eased and became less tense.

Trizonia
The name given to the British, US and French zones of Germany once they merged in 1949.

Truman Doctrine
A policy adopted by the USA after it was announced by President Truman in 1947. It outlined the USA's commitment to supporting democratic nations and peoples anywhere in the world under threat from communism. In practice this meant containing communism and stopping its spread.

Tsar Bomba
The nickname given by the West to a bomb detonated by the USSR in 1961. This Hydrogen bomb was the largest ever to have been exploded.

U2
A spy plane developed by the USA with the ability to fly to an altitude of 70,000 feet, supposedly above the range of defences. Carried a high-resolution camera for surveillance.

United Nations
A multilateral organisation formed in 1945 that attempted, much like the League of Nations, to solve international disputes and encourage global peace and prosperity. Still in existence today.

USSR
Union of Socialist Soviet Republics. The official name of the Soviet Union. The USSR was supposedly a collection of different republics, although in practice they were all centrally run from Moscow.

Viet Cong
Colloquial term derived from contracting the name Viet Nam Cong-san. Used pejoratively by the government of South Vietnam and the US to refer to the Liberation Army of South Vietnam, which was attempting to overthrow the government from within the south.

Viet Minh
The shortened name for the Viet Nam Doc lap Dong minh, Hoi which was a nationalist liberation army led by Ho Chi Minh that fought to liberate Vietnam from foreign interference.

War of Ideas
The Cold War could be said to be a 'war of ideas' at its heart. The USA and the USSR sought to promote their core ways of life abroad through strategic planning and winning of the 'hearts and minds' of people.

Warsaw Pact
A counterpoint to NATO, the Warsaw Pact was an organisation formed in 1955 that served as a defensive pact between the communist states of Eastern Europe. It would, however, be used against one of its members - Czechoslovakia - in 1968.

Western Bloc
A term used to describe the states aligned with the United States during the Cold War.

OTHER WORKS BY VERSUS HISTORY

Amazon Bestseller:
An Infographic History of Germany, 1918-45

Amazon Bestseller:
33 Easy Ways to Improve Your History Essays:

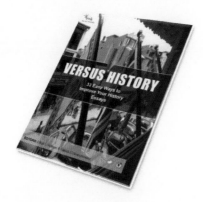

Amazon Bestseller:
Blowing up the Nazis: What you didn't know will blow your mind:

University History Essays (and how to write them)

Lord Durham and the Canada Question:

Don't forget our **Versus History Podcast**, available from wherever you download your podcasts, and our **blog** at www.VersusHistory.com.

Versus History are Dr. Elliott L. Watson, Conal Smith and Patrick O'Shaughnessy.

Published by New Spur Publishing

Websites
www.versushistory.com
www.thecourseworkclub.com

Twitter:
@VersusHistory
@thelibrarian6
@prohistoricman

Instagram:
versushistory

Printed in Great Britain
by Amazon

35450355R00091